DEDICATION

This work is dedicated to my Mother, Brothers and Sisters, and my UE101 Family, and especially to the Urban Underserved Students throughout Our Great Nation. *Wherefore seeing we also are compassed about with so great a cloud of witnesses, let us lay aside every weight, and the sin which doth so easily beset us, and let us run with patience the race that is set before us . . . .*

— (Hebrews 12:1)

MISSION

UNLEASHING THE ACADEMIC
POTENTIAL IN
URBAN SCHOOLS

TABLE OF CONTENTS

The Eight Fundamental UE101 Program Implementations 88

Putting it all together 160

Glossary of UE101 Terms: 167

Endnotes 175

A Restorative Justice Model

When strength is yoked with justice,
where is a mightier pair than they?
— Aeschylus

PROLOGUE

Urban Essentials 101 (UE101) is a school-wide climate and culture stabilization process. It contains programs, practices, and strategies that have been successfully implemented in numerous urban, mostly underserved, districts and schools throughout California for more than a decade. Most of the results have been astonishing. The UE101 process is based upon principles of Restorative Justice (RJ) in School Communities. As such, instead of being identified and cast in the role of perpetrators, receiving punishment for their infractions, students are viewed as valuable members of the campus and community, and their infractions as breaches in the harmonious equilibrium of the climate and culture. Accordingly, the process seeks to identify the relationship breach and restore the balance. It is this fundamental departure that uniquely positions schools using this process to make a positive transition in philosophy, practice, and above all, student progress.

The success of the UE101 process is achieved by aligning and implementing core RJ principles as normalized school practice. The principles are infused into an approach centered upon ensuring that a balance is struck between the site's relationships and available resources. It is this relationship and resources balance that fosters stabilization of the climate and culture. This pairing is then applied to three areas—the site's people, programs, and posture. When these entities (all of which will be explored in greater detail later) are appropriately developed and nurtured, they become the catalyst for the development of a positive, normalized school environment.

This book explains the UE101 process. It offers interventions and strategies along with suggestions for a successful implementation at your school site. The book begins with an explanation and exploration into the origin of the process. It then provides a brief overview of the current predicament or breach in education. From there, it goes on to dispel some of the debilitating myths about urban student success. It ends by providing a clear-cut pathway to the creation of a sustainable climate of safety and a culture of learning and achievement.

ORIGINS OF THE UE101 PROCESS

... A Quick Overview of the UE101 Process

Although all the process components will be discussed in greater detail throughout the book, I believe it is important to provide a thumbnail sketch of the implementation from the start. If you are already familiar with the UE101 plan and only need the strategy for implementation, you may want to proceed to the section on Putting It All Together. Otherwise, the overview is guaranteed not to disappoint.

The UE101 process implementation is referred to as the Urban School Improvement Plan (USIP). The plan contains four (4) operational domains—the framework, the overarching principles, the inputs, and the implementations. The graphic that follows highlights these domains:

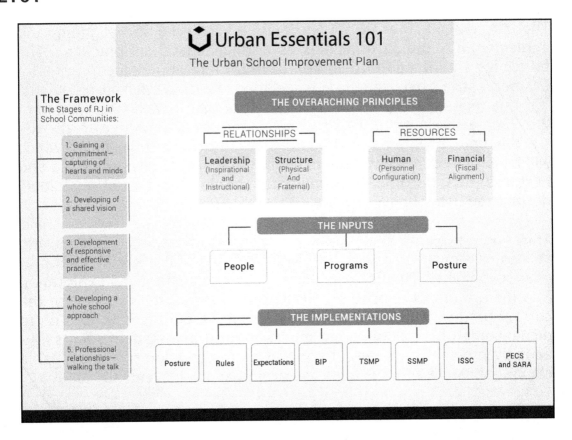

The first domain is the framework. The framework provides the direction and structure for the implementation. It consists of, and is drawn from, the Five Stages of Restorative Justice in School Communities—gaining commitment, developing a shared vision, development of a responsive and effective practice, developing a whole school approach, and professional relationships. The philosophy and stages, as stated, will be discussed in greater detail later. For now, it is sufficient to be aware that the plan is based on the stages.

The next domain consists of the overarching principles. The overarching principles use the framework as a structural touchstone. The guiding principles for the fulfillment of the framework are relationships and resources. It is through the balancing and deployment of these principles that the foundation for the plan is established. Under the overarching principles banner are the main beliefs and practices. They lead directly to the establishment of the plan's inputs and implementations. For example, under the relationship banner resides leadership and structure. Leadership is subdivided into two categories: inspirational and instructional leadership. This understanding of, and desire for, identifying, developing, and promoting inspirational and instructional leaders, assists in the determination process for school site staff placement.

The third domain is the inputs. The inputs are the concrete or physical amenities at a school site. They include the people, programs, and school posture. Their determination is guided by the overarching principles. For example, the teachers—people—selected for a designated school site will possess the inspirational and instructional skills and traits needed for success at that particular school. The same would hold true for the programs being put into practice.

The final domain consists of the implementations themselves. The implementations draw their impetus from the previous domains. On a consistent basis, every individual school site should deploy at least eight (8) universal program implementations. Those implementations include a school posture, common rules, expectations, and a schoolwide behavior intervention plan. Each school should also have a teacher-student mediation program, a student-student mediation program, an in-school suspension classroom program, and a campus-wide internal problem resolution process known as the PECS and SARA Program. PECS stands for problem, effect, cause, and solution. SARA is the acronym for survey, analysis, response, and assessment. The two work together to resolve issues such as physical-plant problems. They might include disruptions, too much trash on the campus, tardiness, or large groups of students congregating in a certain restroom. The process could also be used for resolving morning traffic problems or general campus repairs.

Putting the framework, overarching principles, inputs, and implementations into action is what this book is all about. The USIP brings together the four (4) domains into a school climate and culture development plan. It is through the incorporation and deployment of these elements that a climate of safety and a culture of learning have the greatest opportunity for creation and sustainability. It is through the creation and sustainability of a climate of safety and a culture of learning that student achievement arises and flourishes. So how did I arrive at this understanding?

… Learning to Lead

A river watering the garden flowed from Eden; from there it was separated into four headwaters. The name of the first is the Pishon; it winds through the entire land of Havilah, where there is gold. The name of the second river is the Gihon; it winds through the entire land of Cush. The name of the third river is the Tigris; it runs along the east side of Ashur. And the fourth river is the Euphrates.[1]
Genesis 2:10 – 14

253 Doane St SW, Atlanta, GA 303

©2014 Google

Google earth

33°43'52.73" N   84°23'47.20" W   elev 1060 ft   eye alt 4327 ft

Theories and theses abound regarding urban public schools, especially when it comes to the reasons for underachievement. Everyone wants to see these schools succeed, and nearly as many believe they have the answer. This belief often leaves districts and schools in the unenviable position of attempting to select the genuine change agent from among a clammering host of program inventors and innovators. As a veteran educator who has seen countless initiatives come and go, I recognize that these exploits often create a fair amount of anxiety and skepticism. In anticipation of the apprehension, it is important to explain why the Urban Essentials 101 process is valid, viable and should be fully embraced. Therefore, I will begin this book by providing some background information and particulars about its origin.

The UE101 philosophy and process was essentially developed over more than 40 years. It began with me and my uncommon urban, underserved experience.

As a youth, I grew up in the urban ghettos of Atlanta, Georgia. Surveying my situation, it did not take long for me to recognize a crucial reality. I was not in the Garden of Eden. It was more like the valley of the shadow of death. In fact, during the mid to late 1960's and 1970's, Atlanta was ranked as one of the most violent cities in the nation.[2] The inset above is a Google Earth image of the exact spot of our house. The neighborhood is called Mechanicsville.[3] It was the setting for the 2006 film, ATL,[4] a film based on the community in the 1980's. In my opinion, the movie depicted a super sanitized version of the neighborhood that I experienced. I have not been there for some time, but from the image it looks as if it hasn't changed much. The Genesis 2 inset provides a great platform for a comparison between Mechanicsville and Eden. Like Eden, Mechanicsville was positioned where multiple headwaters or, in this case, busy intersections came together. Instead of flowing rivers where gold could be found, there was a sea of noisy train tracks, highways, a huge junkyard, and machine shops. The machine shops were later used as the location of a cannibal colony called Terminus, in the Walking Dead series.

Directly across the street from our house was London Iron and Metal Company, a mega junkyard. On the eastside, down the block, was bustling Pryor Road, which parallelled the even busier Interstate Highway 75/85. They all converged near University Avenue which pointed the way to the legendary George Washington Carver Vocational High School, my high school.

The junkyard was filthy; it smelled of molten metal and burning rubber, and it smoked and smoldered all day long. Our little house was white, but because of the various airborne particulates from the junkyard, it always had a sooty-gray hue. The soot was so thick that if you wiped it away with a damp cloth today, it would be replenished by tomorrow. In many ways, Mechanicsville and the junkyard were perfectly matched. Like the junkyard, the majority of the citizens of Mechanicsville would probably have been viewed by mainstream America as society's waste and castoffs. The violence and destruction that permeated the neighborhood were ever present. I once attempted to write about all of the young people who died during my childhood. I gave up that depressing task after I had completed a full page of typed names.

In a perverted socio-psychological sort of way, the neighborhood dynamics were actually interesting. We had a few productive citizens; however, the community was dominated by unproductive types. There were bootleggers, drug dealers, pimps, prostitutes, burglars, robbers and thieves, and their clients. I must admit, after my parents separated, we participated in some of those activities as well. My mother was a bootlegger. One of my siblings went to prison for murder; another was a fairly big time drug dealer and pimp. True confession, I was a petty burglar and a needs-based armed robber. But there was something else, my dad.

Strangely enough, my dad was a down-home Southern Baptist Preacher. He was also the eternal optimist. Even with the junkyard as a backdrop, he remained jovial and hopeful. My mother was a single mom of three sons, and 30 years his junior, when they met. It was not a match made in heaven. She was a young, attractive, petty hustler. They separated when I was seven.

After their separation, on Friday evenings, come hell or high water, my dad picked me up. So during the week, I got to be a bona fide hoodrat, but on the weekends I was better travelled than Jesus and the Apostles. From my dad I learned the importance of "real discipline—discipleship." He never gave up. He was the counter measure for Mechanicsville.

At every level of my primary education, I attended segregated schools. Although the 1954 Brown v. BOE of Topeka, Kansas verdict had been rendered, the jury was still out in the Atlanta Public Schools. I started elementary school in 1962 and graduated high school in 1975. In all of those years, there were no Hispanics, and I can only recall one white student who attempted to "break the color barrier." In the span of less than a week, he was shamefully treated, then disappeared.

My high school principal and the overwhelming majority of teachers were also black. However, there were a few exceptions. Some of those were Mr. Christman in Food Service Prep, Mr. Erikson, an old silver-haired, Norwegian-accented guy who taught Drafting and Industrial Arts, and Coach Canard, a crew cut, jar-head type. They managed to stay the course. For the most part, however, white teachers were like ghosts—you saw them for a little while and then they were gone. We were so segregated that I didn't officially meet an Asian or Hispanic student until college. I was so diversity deficient that the first time I met a Hispanic girl face to face, I mistook her for some sort of wacky mulatto mixture. It wasn't until I heard her speak that I cognitively realized that I had to reconstruct my perception of race. Up until then,

I thought in terms of black and white.

Beyond the segregation, all the schools I attended were also dangerous. And with a combination of traits like dangerous, segregated, and urban poor, it would stand to reason that the school also underperformed.

Interestingly enough, back then, I felt sorry for the teachers. Most of them were undoubtedly subject qualified and curriculum ready. The problem, as far as I could see, was not about their content competence; the problem was that they seldom got a chance to deliver it. In most cases, the climate was so horrific that it was not remotely conducive to teaching. As a result, the teachers rarely had an opportunity to demonstrate their instructional prowess.

A big part of the climate problem appeared to come courtesy of the notorious Carver Homes Housing Project. The complex skirted along the southeast edge of the school. Although the spillover was immense, I can't blame the housing project for my poor behavior. I was a legendary knucklehead long before I arrived at Carver High School. In fact, I started receiving suspensions as early as kindergarten. By 1971, I had missed so much school due to suspension for bad behavior and ditching that I was retained in the ninth grade. I always joke about the ninth grade being my best two years of high school, but repeating that year was the least of my issues. I was a ticking timebomb. I was the little clown sitting in class with a stolen gun tucked in his waistband.

Coming from Mechanicsville, we all believed it was imperative to protect ourselves. One day at Carver, it all came to a head. One of my brothers came to me and borrowed "the piece," as he called it. Then, with my gun, he promptly went onto campus and shot two students who were giving him grief. After the dust from the shooting finally settled, a "random search" was held in one of my classes, and I was taken into custody for carrying a knife on campus. The way I saw it was simple. I had no other alternative; Carver was dangerous and they had already confiscated my gun.

I know that my family was out of control. But I make no apologies for our behavior, because we were not the biggest Bozos in this circus. Violence and discord were rampant in my community and at my high school. Things were so bad that our high school queen was murdered. My best friend, a premiere shooting guard and star running back, was eventually sent to death row for murder and armed robbery.

Years later, people still ask me why I didn't go down the same path. My short answer is "I did." I walked the path. The real question, however, is why did I come back? That answer is slightly more complex.

The truth of the matter is this. It's hard for urban knuckleheads to make a course change. Why? Because on some level, the "hood life" is exciting. It is truly a way of life. And if that's all you know, that's all you embrace and do. In my case, however, there was something more compelling than ghetto life. I was blessed with a series of people who were far more inspirational than the everyday drama.

Besides my dad, the greatest inspirational leaders in my life were a couple of legendary teachers—Mr. Charles Henry Banks and Coach C. C. Jones.

In elementary school, Mr. Banks was "the man." I knew about him before I started kindergarten. My brothers gave me the serious lowdown on him. They told me not to even think about trying to run my weak little hoodrat games on him. I later coined a term for teachers like Mr. Banks. I call them "Campus Legends." They are the larger than life characters that everybody, even parents, are aware of. No one seemed to know what they did to gain their status, but everyone knew to take heed.

Mr. Banks was the ultimate inspirational and instructional leader. He wore creased dress-pants, a crisply pressed shirt, a tie, and shined shoes every day. He had duke-inspired wavy hair and a full grille before they became fashionable. Everything I know about science, I learned in the sixth grade from Mr. Banks. He seem to understand that inspiration preceded instruction. He made the funniest jokes and employed a wicked crossover dribble and jumpshot in basketball. He also possessed another trait— fierceness. When needed, he literally, and legally, put a serious butt-whipping on us.

One of my earliest school memories was being sent to Mr. Banks for a butt-whipping. When my third grade teacher had her fill of warnings and no self correction by me, she lived up to her threat and sent me to see him. When I walked into the room, Mr. Banks was lecturing his class. The thing that struck me about it was that everybody was quiet. I locked eyes with my brother (the one who would later become the high school shooter). He was a sixth or seventh grader at the time. From the look in his eyes, I immediately realized that I was in serious trouble. Without stopping his lecture, Mr. Banks pointed to the coat room. I turned and entered. It felt like I was in there for an hour. It was cold, and the lights were turned off. The little light that entered the room came through the window and the cracked door. The light from the window landed on an old 1950's style wooden student deskchair in the middle of the room. After giving his class some parting instructions, Mr. Banks entered the room.

"You are not going to act up anymore," he said. I said "okay." He then said "Lean over that chair." Although I had never done it before, I was a quick study. His last comment was, "And you better not let it go." To this day, I don't know where he got the strap from. I don't remember how many times he hit me because after one, it was a blur. I do, however, remember one thing. Mr. Banks swatted my butt so hard with that first lick, I felt like I was high. Before he entered the room, I had planned to prove my manhood by enduring whatever came my way. After one swat, I forgot all about that crap. I cried like I was at a funeral. When it was over, Mr. Banks told me to pull myself together before I came out. I must have stayed there for ten or fifteen minutes. When I finally walked out, I caught my brother's eyes again, and he was sitting there crying for me. Thereafter, I still acted a fool, but when the threat of Mr. Banks was issued, I stopped. In the end, I became something like Mr. Banks' teacher's pet or probably more like one of his groupies. I could tell that he thought I was pretty smart, and he intended to pull it out of me one way or the other.

Without a doubt, Mr. Banks was one of the primary influences that eventually led me away from a career in crime and to a career in education. For certain, he is the sole reason I wore creased pants, a clean, pressed shirt, a tie and shined shoes for almost two decades while working in schools. The way I saw it, it was the least I could do to pay homage to such an iconic figure. Who knew, it also turns out to be a research-based best practice for climate building. According to a 2009 Southern Illinois Carbondale study, the teacher's appearance and dress is more important than what the teacher is trying to academically discuss.[5] Mr. Banks was the guy who inspired me to listen long enough to be convinced that academic knowledge was a powerful and positive thing. He also helped me to understand that it was alright to be in conflict with the neighborhood "cool" standard. Mr. Banks shaped my belief that inspiration precedes instruction.

In high school, everyone's hero, mine included, was Coach Calvin Coolidge Jones. He preferred CC Jones. His wife and a few select friends (I wasn't in that circle,) got to call him "Monk." If Mr. Banks was legendary, Coach CC Jones was epic. Coach Jones played college basketball at the famed Tuskegee Institute, and he was inducted into the university's athletic Hall of Fame in 1974. His career basketball coaching record, most of it spent at Carver, was 886 wins and 224 losses. He also won the first racially-integrated Georgia State basketball championship in 1967. He was inducted into the SIAC Sports Hall of Fame in 1998 and the Atlanta Sports and Georgia Coaches Hall of Fame in 2009. In 1975, the year I graduated from Carver, our basketball team was so successful (23 and 3) that nearly everybody, even Coach Jones, went off to college. Coach Jones became the first black assistant coach at the University of Georgia.

My relationship with Coach Jones began outside of the classroom. In the fall of 1973, he saw me playing touch football with a group of ditching knuckleheads. I saw him watching, and because of his legendary status, I wanted to showboat for him. After making a what I thought to be a circus-type catch, he called me over. In his high pitched, shrill, but clearly authoritarian voice, he clapped twice and slightly doted over the catch. Then he switched reels and asked me the obvious, "Why are you not in class?" I don't even know what excuse I gave. He then asked me to walk with him. While walking me to the office for being truant, he convinced me to try out for the junior varsity football team.

I made the squad as the starting fullback. We won every game that year. After one of the games, Coach Jones pulled me aside and encouraged me to try out for junior varsity basketball at the end of the season. I made the squad and started at small forward. Thereafter, he took me under his wing and guided me through the rest of high school. Coach Jones gave me his ultimate trust and held me fully accountable for any responsibility lapses or lackadaisical attitude that he detected. By the time he was done running his head game on me, I was a starting varsity player in football and basketball. I also worked so hard academically that I was skipped from the 10th to the 12th grade.

By my senior year, it was clear to all my peers that I was the trusted one. Coach Jones trusted me so much that he made me the designated team taxi driver. It was not at all unusual for him to call me out of class on game day, give me the keys to his car, and send me out into the community to round up my less responsible teammates. He would say, "Take the keys to the *Toyota Baby* and go get the rest of 'em." He would also give me money to buy us food, and say something like, "Make sure they have a real meal before tipoff." I must have gone to every hood, haunt, and housing project in Atlanta looking for some of those guys. But I always came through.

I was so disciplined (in the biblical sense of discipleship) by Coach Jones that the guys mocked, harassed, and called me his son. However, whenever those same guys wanted to go somewhere that required transportation and financial assistance, they knew they had better hunt me down before going to Coach Jones.

As a senior, I was not the MVP in any sport. We had so many great athletes, I wasn't even second, third or fourth runner up. However, at our sports banquet I did receive a trophy. In comparison to the other colossal trophies issued that night, it was a small thing. But to me, it meant everything. The coaches called it the Floor General's Award. The trophy was obviously created just for me. It was for leadership in the intangibles—motivation, trust, dependability, and hustle. It fit me perfectly. And I still have it.

I was Mr. Intangible. I set the tone and bearing or, as I have come to call it, the posture for the team. In short, while the coaches built the culture—teaching us how to play the game—I helped control the climate—the environment or atmosphere necessary for the teaching and learning to occur. As stated, many of our athletes went on to become big time NCAA players; unfortunately, none of them graduated. I ended up playing NAIA football at Culver-Stockton College, formerly Christian University, a Disciples of Christ affiliate, in Canton, Missouri. After three years, I transferred to Georgia State University. I persevered to the end and graduated. Looking back, Coach Calvin Coolidge Jones taught me the value of encouragement, but more importantly, he taught me the value of establishing a viable climate and culture through inspirational and instructional leadership.

After college and graduate school, of all things, I became a police officer. Go ahead, laugh out loud. It was the most unlikely career choice imaginable. But not really.

... Career Choices, Policing, and VORP

I policed with the Fulton County (GA) Police Department from August of 1986 through November of 1995. I must confess that besides teaching, it was easily my all-time favorite occupation. When I took the job, however, that wasn't the case. Entering the field, I had one thought in mind—work four years and get the hell out. After all, they were the police, and being from Mechanicsville, we were taught to hate them. With that kind of attitude about it, one might wonder why was I there in the first place? I had limited options.

As an undergraduate, I was introduced to a governement grant/loan forgiveness program called Law Enforcement Education Program (LEEP). LEEP was giving money to students who majored in Criminal Justice related fields. As a ghetto savvy kid, I couldn't resist the temptation of a deal like that. I saw it as a way to get some free money without the direct confrontation involved in robbery. So I promptly changed my college majors from Art and Physical Education to Administration of Justice and PE. It wasn't until after I started policing that I discovered I really liked the work, and amazingly I was pretty good at it.

What I loved about policing were the same things I loved about teaching— the hands-on interaction with people, the opportunity to forge positive relationships, and the possiblity of making a difference in the community. I think it had something to do with growing up poor in the hood and with an old Baptist preacher. I understood the rules of engagement in the streets, and didn't like them. And at some point, with the ghetto somewhat in the rearview mirror, I started to really believe that I could make things better for people. I actually believed that I could protect and serve. So let's hear it for my dad, Mr. Banks, and Coach CC Jones. Mission accomplished.

Fortunately for me, the type of mentoring I had received along with the ghetto skills I had developed and brought to policing (and later to teaching), were the same skills that were required to perform the work effectively. In an urban underserved environment, in order to be an effective police officer or teacher, one must be able to provide inspirational leadership, clear instructions, and an organized approach. It was a natural fit for me. Taking it a step further, I also understood both sides of the street. I could identify with the underserved community and, with all of the extra academic and social education, I had a decent understanding of the middle class value system as well. The unfamilarity between teachers and urban students is one of the greatest barriers to closing the achievement gap. This assertion will be discussed in greater detail later.

True confesson II: As a police officer, I spent the overwhelming majority of my hours slacking off rather than working. In college, I had developed a fascination for reading about history, and I also became an avid Bible reader. So during the slack time, which could sometimes be hours, I would sit in my patrol car and read history, government, economics, and religious textbooks for fun. Because I was, and continue to be, a pretty slow reader, I never had time to read and appreciate fiction; therefore, there was no genre competition. Not only did I love reading, but I also got into the nuances of translation and became a researcher of sorts. I read the King James Version of the Bible from cover to cover. Then in order to get different perspectives, I read the New International Version, The Living Bible, and one called simply called The Book. Wanting to go a little deeper, I deviated from Bible translations to other spiritual books. I read the Book of Mormon, The Quran, Watchman Nee's The Spiritual Man, The Complete Works of Josephus, Halley's Bible Handbook, and even the Unger's Bible Dictionary.

After about a decade of reading, I began to feel a wave of dissatisfaction. Soon thereafter the day arrived when I had to ask myself a tough question. Was it time to move on? I ended up not having to make the decision; circumstances called the shot. The tipping point came when I had what I will call a legal dispute (although I really believed it to be a more of an ethical and spiritual challenge) with my department. A three-year federal court battle ensued, and when the dust settled, the courts sided with me. After the affirming decision, I resigned and moved to Fresno, California.

In January of 1996, I took a job with the Victim Offender Reconcilation Program (VORP). It was at VORP that I found my true social philosophy, ideology, and calling: Restorative Justice. VORP of the Central Valley was a program that primarily operated as a collaborative with the Fresno County Juvenile Probation Department. The collaboration was rather straightforward. Prior to appearing before a judge for final adjudication, or as part of the final resolution, a case could be referred to VORP for a mediated agreement.

VORP brought victims of crimes face to face with juvenile offenders in hopes of facilitating an agreement that could include the following: relational restoration, reconciliation, and, if required, restitution. VORP was unquestionably devoted to and founded upon principles of Restorative Justice (RJ).

RJ has recently become one of the buzzwords in education. In many cases, however, I believe that its full potential is not being exploited. So, what is Restorative Justice? RJ is an administrative theory of law enforcement that emphasizes repairing the societal harm caused by criminal or deviant behavior. The work of RJ is generally achieved through a cooperative procedure that includes the persons directly affiliated with and affected by the crime—the victim, the offender, and ultimately the larger community. Some of the program components identified as forms of RJ include:

» Victim-offender mediation
» Conferencing
» Circles
» Victim assistance
» Ex-offender assistance
» Restitution
» Community service [6]

(And since 1999, in schools) Urban Essentials 101

Ron Claassen, Professor Emeritus of Peacemaking and Conflict Studies, School of Education at Fresno Pacific University (FPU) is a pioneer in RJ and the founder of VORP of the Central Valley. I was fortunate to be selected and directly trained in the VORP process by him. From Mr. Claassen's perspective, and I concur, the Criminal Justice (CJ) System by and large discourages reconciliation. Under the guise of protecting society from a perpetrator, in many cases the CJ system actually creates more alienation and anxiety. He explained how retaliation, retribution, reprisal, and revenge can actually hurt the victims as much as the offenders, while reconciliation and restoration can heal both. No doubt, VORP facilitates community restoration.

Upon completion of the VORP training, I was certified as a mediator. The culminating event in the VORP mediation process was to personally mediate at least three cases. Before leaving the organization, I mediated or assisted in the completion of at least 1,000 cases. I also managed over 300 volunteer mediators and assisted in their training.

Under the VORP banner, I also interfaced monthly with officials from the Fresno County Probation Department. My primary duty as liaison was to secure cases for the VORP mediation process. With my law enforcement background, developing a rapport with the probation staff and securing cases was a cinch. We got so many that we had to ask them to slow down on the referrals.

My office was in the College Community Church, a Mennonite Brethren institution, in Clovis, CA. It was from that location that I managed, monitored and, when needed, co-mediated to ensure that the most suitable and sustainable reconciliation and resolution were achieved. The resolutions forged were founded upon the three fundamental RJ principles: recognizing of the injustice, restoring equity to the best extent possible, and establishing clear future relationship expectations. In short, we gave the people most directly affected by the transgression—the victim and offender—a venue to be heard, some relief (psychological and/or material), and a peaceful pathway to the future.

At VORP, I saw juvenile offenders and their victims laugh together, cry together, become friends, and even develop working relationships that continued well beyond the completion of the mediation process. On one occasion, I knew of a community grocery store owner who hired and mentored his offender after the youth had burglarized and vandalized his store. Seeing so many positive outcomes, I couldn't help but believe in and embrace the initiative. (For more information about VORP, visit their website at www.vorp.org.)

... Teacher Credentialing

Everything was going well at VORP until Roberta (Bobbi) Jentes Mason and Mary Ann Larson-Pusey showed up. Mason and Larson-Pusey were professors in the FPU Teacher Education Program. In no time, they convinced or more like Mennonite strong-armed me into believing that there was potentially another calling on my life.

The professors, who in their spare time were VORP mediators, had heard about me and my experiences growing up in the inner-city of Atlanta. Even though things were going great at VORP, they were convinced that my talents could be better utilized elsewhere. They believed that I was uniquely suited for teaching "urban underserved students" (a term that I first heard articulated by Dr. Mason). The two were relentless in their pursuit and eventually won outright. The defining moment for them, and me, came in the summer of 1996.

Each summer, the professors directed a program created by Dr. Mason called The Learning Edge Project. Learning Edge promoted and reinforced the importance of literacy for urban underserved high school youth. That summer, I was asked to speak to a group of student participants about my life and the transformation that ultimately changed my trajectory. In a debriefing following the discourse, the professors were practically giddy with enthusiasm. According to them, the presentation was riveting. They went on to convey that the students were totally engaged. Naïve me, I thought that engagement was a natural byproduct of effective communication. If I could communicate the lecture by way of their experience, why wouldn't they be engaged? It just happened to be another opportunity for me to speak about both sides of the street— the hood and the good. What I did not know was that the climate in many urban underserved schools had become so dysfunctional that the behavior demonstrated by those summer students was noteworthy.

Shortly after the presentation, I enrolled in the FPU teacher credentialing program. I continued to work at VORP during the day while attending evening classes. The teacher education experience was an eye-opener right from the start.

My first educational epiphany came almost immediately. I discovered that I didn't view education in quite the same way as the overwhelming majority of my cohorts. On a macrolevel we agreed. We all believed education to be the great societal equalizer, and we also shared a similar passion for kids. We even agreed that the privilege of attaining a quality education should rate right up there with constitutional rights.

However, the difference we had was on a micro-level. Our fundamental parting of the ways came in how that privilege should be promoted and disseminated. Ironically, I was usually the most conservative voice.

My general thinking around the topic was this. If education on a macro-level is a privilege, on a micro-level we ought to act like it. The dominant opinion among my peers, however, was different. They seemed to think that urban underserved students didn't quite understand the privilege, so we needed to make exceptions and patiently teach them to appreciate it. I thought that position was a crock of frigging crap. I believed then, and I still do, that that type of thinking is dangerous and detrimental. It is that type of micro-thinking that places us (the educational system) on the path of giving urban underserved students a free pass and/or an excuse for low expectations and low performance. In my opinion, low expectations and excuses for low performance are the culprits of the achievement gap, not teacher academic ineptness.

Why does this free pass and low expectation nonsense persist throughout the micro-climate? I think it is because most of my cohort members (just as a great many of the decision makers in education today) view the dilemma through middle-class lenses. Although they mean well and have good intentions, the urban underserved experience is usually not a part of their standard repertoire. Therefore, when they make decisions, they draw their impetus from their own experiences and frames of reference. Their hearts are in the right place, but their research is off base. Compassion and understanding are two different things. After a while, it starts to look like trying to remedy the plight of a freezing junkyard dog by putting him in a sweater knitted for a Beverly Hills pampered poodle.

Frankly, I think the issue is capacity related, but not academic capacity. I believe this to be the reason for the predicament. So few people in the educational leadership elite come from life experiences like those of the urban underserved that their needs are virtually impossible to understand. Therefore, as mentioned, they (the leadership elite) often end up responding to the urban underserved from the only frame of reference available: their own and that of their common cohort. It creates limited perspective. A good example of this limited perspective was expressed to me by a member of my teacher education cohort.

Unlike most of my teacher education cohorts, this colleague and I had come into education much later in life. I was 39 years old; he was even older. I think it was the age factor that drew us close enough to respectfully share ideas. After several conversations on the topic, I could hear a slight shift in his perspective.

One day, while discussing the issue, he made a very relevant observation. It was rooted in his college experience, more than twenty years earlier. After giving him my patented spiel on the educational dilemma, my colleague said, "I think you might be onto something. There was something missing." He went on to say that he had been thinking about the topic as it related to a dear friend from college. My colleague, who happened to be white, had made friends with a black male student who was from an urban underserved community. The relationship that they shared, according to my colleague, was excellent. They grew so close that the guy had even been a member of his wedding entourage. Then with a look of adoration on his face, he went on to say that he loved the guy. That's when the Aha moment came! As his expression changed from adoration to perplexed reflection, he said despairingly, "but there was always something missing." According to him, something seemed to hinder the next step in the relationship, something that prevented a full connection. He then said, in a matter-of-fact tone, that the something was not race. And I would concur. It was not race: it was the experiential understanding.

... It's all about the Relationship, Not Race

The something my colleague felt was a lack of experiential understanding, sometimes called a lack of background knowledge. My colleague was from a middle class rural environment, and his friend came from an urban underserved experience. When he made his declaration, I fully understood what he meant. In fact, while in college I had similar experiences in reverse. In college, I met several other black students who had been raised in middle and upper-class environments, whether urban or rural. We were all black, but could not become extremely close because we could not fully identify with the experience of the other. It was not their blackness that helped or hindered our relationship; it was the different environmental experience. Race was immaterial. (Later, we will look at our teaching force as it relates to environmental upbringing and experience.) The breach, as I call it, wasn't of the heart; it was an experiential chasm. It wasn't enough to stop heartfelt friendships from developing, but it was enough to stave off a more complete understanding between us. As youth in college, over the years we lived close enough to one another and interacted intimately enough, to accept, ignore and/or overcome the basic effects of the breach. We exchanged ideas and modified our beliefs enough to allow friendships to flourish. Thereafter, on some level, we could become inspirational and instructional with one another.

In urban primary and secondary school settings, however, without the basic understanding that was allowed to flourish in college, an inspirational and instructional achievement gap tends to emerge. The simplest way for me to say this is: if you don't understand something about the urban underserved, it is difficult to inspire them, and if you can't inspire them, it will be extremely difficult, if not impossible, to instruct them. It's about the relationship, not race.

In many urban underserved districts, as with my teacher education colleague, we know that something is amiss. Low achievement and disruptive behavior make it abundantly clear. What seems to escape us is what is causing the predicament. We cannot and will not do better if we continue to reduce the problem to spurious variables such as poor instruction and racism. Generally speaking, teachers know the content material they teach. However, because erroneous variables, like quality instruction and race, are such politically charged subjects, the tendency is to migrate towards them, in order to satisfy constituencies. Then the bandwagon effect takes hold, and urban education is off for another four or five year stint down one more rabbit hole.

After settling on the variables, a host of well-intended educational leaders, philosophers, researchers and pundits then direct their efforts and our financial resources towards them. Programs are geared toward materials and professional developments designed to advance instructional improvement, curriculum development and more recently, cultural proficiency—which in most cases means race relations.

One of the best explanations for this phenomenon I have heard was espoused by the late Georgia State University Educational Psychologist, Dr. Asa Hilliard.[7] Several years ago, while attending an African American Educators conference in San Diego, California, I heard Dr. Hilliard refer to the phenomenon as the "Illegitimate Legitimacy." He went on to assert that the educational elite reach and follow illegitimate conclusions based on the preeminence of their own research. Then, directives and direction are set based on those ideas. Because of this behavior, we often end up with underdeveloped or shortsighted initiatives, which later manifest themselves as flawed programming, which in turn leads to the unjustified validation of a false narrative [8]—poor teacher quality and racism.

The No Child Left Behind Act is a perfect example of the false narrative. As reauthorization of the Elementary and Secondary Education Act of 1965, NCLB became US law in 2001.[9] Using a football analysis, NCLB moved the ball, but it didn't change the thinking about the game. Instead of focusing on a micro-level—inspirational and relational, the focus appeared to be on the macro-perspective—resource distribution and implementation side of the equation—resources (mainly quality instruction). The system was built on, and aligned with, the illegitimate legitimacies—content standards, high-stakes testing, and penalties for not meeting the standards. Eventually, because of a lack of improvement, the NCLB conversation was reduced to demands for high quality teachers, charter schools, and vouchers, and left to wither into obscurity. If we do not change our thinking, I suspect we will see the same outcome with Common Core State Standards (CCSS), Race to The Top, and the current Every Student Succeeds Act (ESSA) which was signed into law by President Obama in 2015.

I am not at all against accountability, standards, and testing. We should be aware of the quality of education being provided by our teachers and the knowledge acquired by our students. The issue for me arises when we formulate our thinking around why learning is not occurring and what to do as a result. The problem is not, and has never been, that we didn't have standards. This line of reasoning, although certainly well-intended, inescapably sets the stage for illegitimate solutions. Enough! So where do we go from here? Urban Essentials 101, of course! But let's take a bit more time getting there.

... A New Path

If you have been in or around the education profession for any length of time, everything I have articulated so far probably sounds like just another dose of Eduspeak—a lot of "Clouds but No Rain." Or as the Sage of the South, also known as the Godfather of Soul, and Soul Brother #1, the late great James Brown would say: "It's Like a Dull Knife, Just Ain't Cuttin, Just Talking Loud but Saying Nothing."

With all of the aforementioned history and policy as a backdrop, the ultimate question that eventually emerges is this. How do I get you (the reader) to trod the beaten path once again? Or more precisely, how do I convince you to take a different path for the first time?

I make no bones about it— my primary goal here is to get you to accept and travel in a new educational direction. The only legal medium I have at my disposal is the power of persuasion. So this time, I bear no weapons, stolen or otherwise obtained, just words. The primary persuasive device this time will be evidence derived from my personal educational experience and research as an educator.

... Teaching, the Early Years

Although I occasionally gained traction with some of my teacher education cohort, for the most part my position remained a minority report. The next school year, however, I got a chance to put some of my theory to the test. While still in the teacher education program, I was encouraged by Mason and Larson-Pusey to attend the FPU Annual Career Fair. One of the participating districts was the Fresno County Office of Education. While talking with their representative, I was encouraged to apply for a teaching position. After passing the CBEST (California Basic Education Skills Test) and securing an Emergency Credential (later converted into an Intern Credential), I interviewed and got hired as a teacher.

My first assignment was incredible. I was assigned to teach Language Arts and Social Sciences at the newly formed, Elkhorn Correctional "Boot Camp" Facility School. While I didn't feel completely prepared instructionally, inspirationally I thought myself to be uniquely qualified. The boot camp was a juvenile facility located in the middle of the desert in Caruthers, California.[10] Fresno County had opened the facility as an alternative adjudication strategy for juvenile offenders. The programming consisted of a discipline regimen that included physical training, counseling and school.[11] I was excited about the job. On another level, however, it felt as if I hadn't fully escaped the Criminal Justice System.

Elkhorn Correctional School and I were another near perfect pairing. The only negative that I could see was the location of the facility itself. The camp was housed inside a decommissioned regional jail, and school was held inside renovated army-style barracks. There were two tall fences, with an approximate 15-foot gap between them that surrounded the camp. Each fence was topped with barbed wire, and an entanglement of razor wire filled the 15-foot no-man's land between them.
The first order of business was to set up the school. With the assistance of a few cadets (as the student inmates were called), we pulled it off in no time.

When the full contingency of cadets arrived, I immediately sensed that I would be able to relate to them without much difficulty. However, I also innately understood that relating to them would have nothing to do with my race.

When the door opened, the cadet leader walked in and asked if I were ready for the students to enter. I don't know why, but I got up, walked over, shook his hand, and acknowledged that I was ready. It was the beginning of a ritual that I continued for the next two decades. As they filed by and received what I called the Right Hand of Fellowship (a term based on Galatians 2:9, and used in black churches throughout the South signifying that you are a welcome participant),[12] I made my first observation. The cadets were not predominantly black; in fact, there were only two or three black students in the entire group. Most the cadets were Hispanic, followed by Southeast Asians—Vietnamese, Cambodians, Laotians, and a group that I had not even heard of until I arrived in Fresno, Hmong. The group was rounded out by a spattering of Pacific Islanders—Samoans and their mortal enemy, Tongans. Just as with black students, there were only a few whites.

In no time at all, however, we were a team and having a blast. My capacity to forge an authentic relationship with the "cadets" was so apparent that the security staff, called Tact Officers, rarely even bothered to drop by to check up on us. I usually saw the officers only at the beginning and end of school, although there were a few who dropped by for their own edification—to listen in on a lesson and/or to swap sordid law enforcement tales with me.

The entire year, Tact Officers came to my room for a behavioral issue only once. And when they did, boy, they really came running. The kid was a new black cadet who felt that he needed to protect himself. He was clearly afraid and flat-out refused to trust in my ability to provide refuge. Immediately he began to deploy the only protection method in his repertoire—signification of his gang affiliation. The lack of trust, as I saw it, most likely stemmed from past school experiences. I tried for almost five minutes, which was about four minutes and thirty seconds too long, to get him to discontinue the behavior and settle down. I even invited him outside for a more private conversation, but he refused.

As it turned out, he was in a pissing contest with another cadet he knew from a rival gang on the streets. In my classroom, he was simply trying to assert his dominance. The only problem I had with that was that it was my classroom and I was already "the man or top dawg" in there. By the time the new cadet arrived, his rival, a Hispanic kid, was already a Mr. Lockett's classroom veteran. He knew the deal and the drill, and he had simply decided to exploit the situation. He taunted the newbie outside of school, then simply chilled and waited for a response once in the classroom. It was a masterful manipulation. Although the newbie and I would eventually develop a great relationship, on that day he had to be whisked away by the Tact Officers for "programming."

Programming included interventions like push-ups, then running around the huge track field that encompassed the inner perimeter of the facility in the blistering August desert sun. The running activity was coupled with the carrying of a car or truck tire overhead, while yelling "I will not disrupt school." One of my all-time favorite consequences—the mud hole—appeared to be reserved for extremely hot days. The mud hole entailed the digging of a deep hole. The dirt that was extracted became a mound alongside the hole. The hole would then be filled with water. I know the knucklehead in you can already see where this is headed. While adorned with the car tire as bling, the cadet had to drag himself through the muddy hole and then over the dirt mound, while yelling the refrain, "I will not disrupt school."

We were not treated to this spectacle often, but when we were, I wouldn't miss the opportunity to make it an objective lesson. As a teacher, I was probably considered a bit unorthodox. I encouraged things like teacher-directed daydreaming for inspiration. If a student was going through the mud-hole or experiencing some other extraneous challenge outside of my classroom window, I wouldn't fight the funk. I wouldn't try to keep the students away from doing something as natural as watching the spectacle. It's normal, and most of us do it. Face it, when you drive past an accident on the freeway, even if it's on the other side of the median wall, you slow down to look. It makes more sense to me to exploit the incident than fight it. I would take the class on a field trip to the window.

My thinking was simple. I was the leader of a potentially inspirational activity that could easily be morphed into a writing workshop. The writing could be persuasive, descriptive, explorative, comparative, or contrasting. Questions like: Explain whether you think the behavior that led to the event was worth it? Describe or explain the process that you observed. Compare this activity with other forms of behavioral consequences that you have observed. Reality prompts should always be exploited. Hell, the six-o'clock news does it all the time.

The first time I saw the Tact-Officers' interventions deployed, I fully understood the rationale. It was all about the forging of a clear understanding about the behavioral expectations, and maintaining the facility's climate of safety. Their thinking was not radically different from the philosophy espoused by my dad, Mr. Banks, and Coach Jones. The only real difference was in the implementation methodology.

For example, on one of my weekend visits with my dad, when he learned I had been messing up in school, I vividly recall him telling me there were only two games in town—fear and respect. He went on to say they usually boiled down to mental or physical consequences. He ended by saying that to make me a better person, he didn't care which he had to use. Initially I felt a little put off by what seemed to be a pretty hard line to take with his "posterity." Later, however, I grew to completely understand his reasoning. He, and the others for that matter, would rather have operated with me out of a position of respect, but if respect wasn't readily achievable, equal enthusiasm would be undertaken to embrace the fear tactic until a suitable climate had been restored. From his perspective, it was okay to employ fear. After all, as a preacher, to him "The fear of the Lord is [was] the beginning of wisdom." (Psalm 111:10). What he and the others understood about the urban underserved youth was that as time passed, the fear would naturally morph into respect. And it did. I raised my son under the same system and he turned out even better than I did. He is a supervising mechanical engineer for National Aerospace Solutions at Arnold Engineering Development Complex, Arnold Air Force Base, in Tennessee where he tests jet engines for a living.

The Tact Officers were implementing a strategy that guaranteed a prompt climate reset. They simply employed a quick climate stabilizer. In my opinion, too many urban underserved schools attempt to operate in a climate devoid of fear or respect for adult leadership.

With this quick fix available, the boot camp school climate was almost instantaneously made ready for a higher level of teaching and learning. After the climate was set, I literally had a captive audience. For certain, this was not the optimum environment for student achievement; however, it was far better than attempting to operate in an environment with no fear or respect. (Of course, I will discuss more about creating an environment that is conducive to teaching and learning later.)

After the environmental climate was established, my job was to get the students to believe in and embrace my instructional practice. The only way to achieve that was by providing the group with enough inspiration to become self-motivated learners. I don't want to get preachy (and I can), but I do want this point to be clear. After a suitable environment has been established, what you do to inspire students is crucial.

I believe in this inspirational component so deeply that more than a decade ago, I created a process to describe the achievement progression. I refer to it as The Urban Education Success Pyramid. The following graphic illustrates the progression.

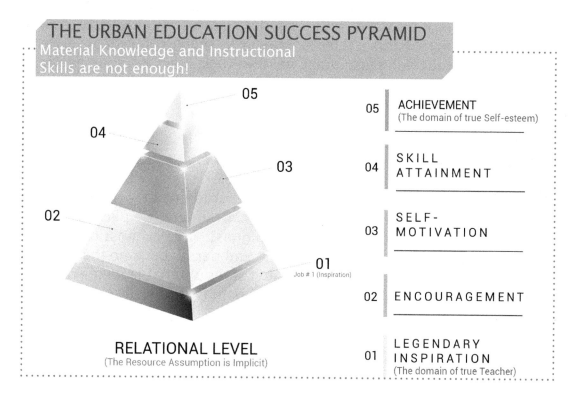

THE URBAN EDUCATION SUCCESS PYRAMID

Material Knowledge and Instructional Skills are not enough!

05	**ACHIEVEMENT** (The domain of true Self-esteem)
04	**SKILL ATTAINMENT**
03	**SELF-MOTIVATION**
02	**ENCOURAGEMENT**
01	**LEGENDARY INSPIRATION** (The domain of true Teacher)

RELATIONAL LEVEL
(The Resource Assumption is Implicit)

Job # 1 (Inspiration)

The number one job of any teacher is to inspire students. The dissemination of information is a distant second. The best way to achieve this is to become what I refer to as a legendary inspirational leader. Inspiration in this case can be defined as having the capacity to convince a student that he or she is safe and can achieve. It all starts with the leadership. The legendary inspirational leaders, and not the knuckleheads, must be the Rock Stars of your campus.

The legendary part takes place over time. Therefore, a legendary inspirational leader is a teacher or staff member who has had several years of affirmative leadership in a community and is idolized by other school affiliates—staff, students, and parents, i.e. Mr. Banks and Coach CC Jones.

The inspirational leader's job is to inspire students enough to become encouraged. And when sufficiently encouraged, students become self-motivated. After becoming self-motivated, skill attainment becomes relatively easy. Lastly, skill attainment is the dynamic that leads directly to achievement. It all starts with legendary inspirational leaders. Again, in order for any of this cycle to transpire, the inspirational leaders, and not the knuckleheads, must be the Rock Stars of your campus.

... Climate and Culture

After several years of working in urban underserved schools, I have observed that in many cases where student behavior was out of control, no reliable climate of safety was established. Without a proper adult-set climate, students attempt to protect themselves. In this self-preservation environment, a pecking order often forms. In the pecking order, the biggest, rudest, most outlandish students, and not the super bookworms and nerds, become the campus leaders. When this occurs, the campus becomes untenable for maximized teaching and learning. Because the staff is fully aware of the situation, and because of district pressures to achieve, a fallacious employment protection scheme sometimes emerges. In the scheme, the staff often brokers a deal with the students. Administrators, by whatever means at their disposal, pressure teachers. Teachers then forge a false narrative about the culture of learning. In Theodore Sizer's book Horace's School, he calls this phenomenon "Playing the game of school." [13]

The game of school is basically a mutual agreement between the teacher and students to produce an on-demand dog and pony show for dignitaries. Here is how the game of school works. When district and/or other affiliates visit the school, students agree to moderate their behavior. Students become more polite, punctual, and cast the appearance of productivity. Conversely, when no dignitaries are around, the students are given near behavioral carte blanche. This does not insinuate that no learning is taking place. In fact, there are genuinely a few higher performing classes on campus, and certain students are directed to those courses. For those students, their part in the conspiracy is to make no waves. In exchange for the protection of their peace and privilege, they comply. For this agreement to occur there must be sacrifices. The sacrificial lambs in this case are quality instruction, genuine learning, and authentic grading. Limited instruction time, lower test scores, and inflated grades are a hallmark of this process. It's essentially a quid pro quo to the detriment of the students.

At some schools, there is a clear "fait accompli." In the aftermath, the serious knuckleheads then get to talk crap and, in the eyes of their peers and some staffers, back it up. When this occurs, most constituencies clam up or, in a worst case scenario, align with the knuckleheads—a form of Stockholm Syndrome. Of course, in either case, as stated, the biggest losers in this process are the students themselves.

Why do you think kids don't "snitch" on other kids? It is not because they admire and love villains. It is more likely to be because they have seen the adage played out or heard the tales about snitches who really got stitches without real consequences.[14]

There are some urban schools that really do attempt to hold the line, but it is usually done through a double down on adult fear tactics. These schools use detentions, suspensions, and expulsions as their stimulus for acquiescence. The problem with these approaches, however, is they are shortsighted and unsustainable. On the shortsighted side, for many urban underserved students, the interventions are not disincentives. There was perhaps a time when a suspension made an urban underserved student feel as though he or she was a disappointment or had shamed the family, resulting in contrition. That attitude, like Father Knows Best and Leave It to Beaver, is a thing of the past. In most cases, sending a student home is, at least in their minds, like banishing them to an oasis. They get to be away from the school madness and, because most parents work, spend the time unsupervised.

Beyond the shortsightedness, the real problem with using detentions, suspensions, and expulsions is they are not inspirational, and therefore not sustainable. You can send disruptive students away all day long. However, until they are 18 years old, they always get to come back. When they do, they are further behind academically and walk in the door with an arrogant posture. In the final analysis, it makes the school officials appear weak and the student bulletproof. And I didn't even venture down the financial track. Suspending and expelling students is like paying your staff to send your money away.

Without a doubt, everyone—parents, students, teachers and other affiliates—wants a school climate and culture that is conducive to teaching and learning, but the clear majority of us don't want a tact officer-style discipline regimen in order to achieve it. If we are not willing to have tact officers in our schools, we need to have better alternative interventions to satisfy the climatic component.

Most fair-minded people would agree that climate precedes culture. (This climate-culture relationship will also be discussed later.) The strategies that will be discussed in this text have been proven to stabilize the climate without the tactical officers' approach.

What I brought to the table at boot camp, and at the eight or so other urban underserved school venues I worked over the decades, was clear—urban background knowledge, the capacity to build inspirational relationships with students, and the ability to implement the needed structures to forge a climate of safety and a culture of learning and achievement.

... Low Expectations, Really

Early on, I had been told by the district's program administrators that I shouldn't expect much out of the boot camp cadets. The recurring refrain was, their skills are low and they are just not able to read and write very well. I thought this was another round of crap. As a youth, I was a very slow reader, but I could read. So I knew better—I had been one of them. Hell, the only thing that kept me out of a boot camp-style program when I was a kid was there wasn't one to send me to. However, I could read. And many of boot camp cadets could also read. They, like me, just didn't get into earnestly reading and writing until inspired to do so. By the end of the year, the majority of students were fully engaged, not just in reading, but in all aspects of school. With the appropriate inspiration, they embraced academic exercises with the same rigorous attitude as students anywhere else. The change was so palpable that I could literally feel the intellectual shift. In less than a year, the students read, and desired to read, so much I ended up creating a reading center in our barrack.

The reading center was crammed full of great books. I must also give props to the Fresno County Office of Education for their support of the project. Our titles included everything from *A Tale of Two Cities and Call of the Wild* to *Count Dracula, and Frankenstein.* For every ten books, we had one version on audiobook. Any kid could use an audiobook, but there were stipulations, of course. If you used an audio book, you had to also follow along with a hard copy. Furthermore, whether audio or not, each student had to keep a log and write an essay at the end. That was a no brainer. I structured the reading log as a scaffold for the essay. (A sample reading log follows.)

Urban School Reading Log

Student: _____   Book Start Date: _____

                                          Date Completed: _____

Book/Magazine Title: _____

Author: _____   Genre: _____   Page Count: _____

Reading Summary and Critique
(The summary and critique must be in paragraph form.)

Entry Date: _____   Number of pages read: from _____ to _____
Summary and Critique:

_____

_____

_____

_____

_____

_____

Entry Date: _____   Number of pages read: from _____ to _____
Summary and Critique:

_____

_____

_____

_____

_____

Entry Date: _____   Number of pages read: from _____ to _____
Summary and Critique:

_____

_____

_____

_____

_____

Continue on back

The cadets loved those books, but their all-time favorite book was a book called *Makes Me Wanna Holler*, by Nathan McCall.[15]

Makes Me Wanna Holler was about the life of a young black man growing up in inner-city America. However, it wasn't his blackness that fascinated them. It was the growing up in urban, inner-city America that captivated the group. It was the fact that Nate was growing up in the streets of Norfolk, Virginia that struck a chord with them. They, and I, could identify with Nate's urban ghetto exploits and his ultimate plight. I knew that I had hit the mark when one of the students said, "I didn't know that you could put this kind of stuff in a book." By the way, just for the record, it was FPU Professor Mary Ann Larson-Pusey, a middle-aged, Midwestern, white woman who introduced me to the book.

I used it as a read aloud. The students loved the book so much they suggested we write the author and tell him so, and we did. We spent the better part of a week writing, editing, revising, and sending our letters of appreciation. The securing of a climate of safety, the lab, and *Makes Me Wanna Holler* were as effective as the toughest Tact Officers in controlling students' harmful behavior. Those guys practically begged me to read, and I'm not the world's best at reading aloud. I consented, but with some serious caveats. I would only read after we finished our other studies. They eagerly complied and made sure the new arrivals did as well.

Although the reading lab was separated from the classroom by an elaborate walled partition, it was crammed full of testosterone-driven, juvenile armed robbers and carjackers, who on the streets claimed to represent different factions and gangs. For the entire year, we didn't have a single fight in the joint and rarely even an argument. When an argument did occur, it was usually about a book. Like real regular students, it was the fear of losing the privileges, my respect, the environment, and the potential peril of no *Makes Me Wanna Holler* that controlled the climate. This ultimately paved the way to a culture of high expectations, which inevitably leads to learning. Snitches didn't get stitches in our school, they got praised.

... San Diego Unified School District

The next year I took a job with the San Diego Unified School District. The boot camp cadets, however, kept me hopping. Until my group of cadets had all cycled through the program, I received a continuous stream of elaborate letters from those guys. One day after reading a couple of their letters, I had another epiphany. I realized that when it came to educating urban underserved students, we were doing something drastically wrong. Besides the "they don't understand the privilege" nonsense, we were selling them short on other fronts. A major front was the "they don't really know how to read and write" myth. As mentioned, they read, wrote, edited and rewrote when they were inspired and had a compelling incentive to do so. Their work wasn't flawless, but nobody's work is perfect. Just like me, because of the turned-off and tuned-out time, there were conventions gaps. However, instead of recognizing and rectifying the gaps, we often ended up making excuses rather than making it a challenge. Excuses always morph into the low-expectation trap. It is this trap that leads to the "dumbing-down" of the work, or as some of the students referred to it, "giving us baby work." Quite frankly, it's an insult to their intelligence, and they know it.

We often lack the ability to build inspirational relationships because we start out with an inferiority premise. We tend to view the issue instructionally as opposed to inspirationally. Instead of working on the relationship component, we begin to develop instructional strategies. Then by default, we go to the illegitimate legitimacy of professional development for poor or struggling readers. Our job is to inspire and instruct. The boot camp brought the importance of the two to the forefront. But again, I reiterate, inspiration precedes instruction. This premise would eventually become the impetus for the development of the UE101 process.

...The Birth of the Program

In 1998, after a terrific year at the boot camp, I accepted a social science teaching position in the San Diego Unified School District. My first assignment was at an infamous alternative school called YOU (Youth Opportunities Unlimited). The school was in the Barrio Logan community of San Diego. The community and the school were overwhelmingly Mexican and extremely high poverty. It was about a half mile walk from the famed Chicano Park, home of our country's largest collection of outdoor murals.[16] Interestingly enough, the murals, which covered the entire park, were primarily painted on the trestles underneath the Interstate Highway 5 Bridge. Along with the late Albert Collins, a fellow teacher, I would power walk to the park three or four times a week as exercise prior to the start of school. Pictures of a few of my favorite murals follow:

Walking through the park, it was clear that Mexican heritage was important, but a closer inspection revealed evidence of another more ominous legacy—gangs. All along the walking route, on utility boxes, fire hydrants, fences and directional markers, traffic signs, and even in strategically prominent spots inside the park, gang graffiti, tags, and placards boldly announced their influence and presence.

YOU consisted of a cluster of six to ten portable classrooms, and like the boot camp, they were surrounded by an eight to ten foot high fence. There was no grass, and I don't recall a single tree. The poor student behavior at YOU clearly reflected the tenor of neighborhood and the school. There was an obvious lack of inspirational leadership and few authentic relationships. It felt destitute and tense.

Although some of the students, just as with any school, were able and awesome, they were severely overshadowed by the bands of knuckleheads and gang wannabes. The kids spent their days posing, posturing, and being profane, while the adults spent their time complaining to one another about the kids. The administration's general response to the bad behavior was so off-target that by the end of the first day, I knew it was going to be nearly impossible for me to be successful. However, I was not one to walk away from a challenge without a fight. So, after couple of months of observation, I took my case directly to the top. I went to the principal for a discussion about my perceptions, assessment, and potential strategies for improvements.

After speaking with the principal, who also happened to be a black man from San Diego, I left even more disillusioned. When I heard his perspective on the situation, I knew that I could not remain there beyond the current year. He obviously felt the same way.

In our meeting, I told him the student behavior was out of control and the constant disruptive drama was ridiculous nonsense. I went on to declare that I believed I could help him do something about the situation. Without hesitation, the guy laughed in my face; then he completely disagreed. According to him, the students were "acting normal." He went on to say that they were simply a byproduct of their environment, and that the bad behavior was "cultural." I almost fainted. Okay, that was a bit of hyperbole. Nevertheless, I really couldn't believe what I was hearing.

The principal, the inspirational leader, believed that ignorance and arrogance were normal. He went on to say that in his opinion, I was more of a problem than the kids. He said I was demanding too much from the students, and I was trying to act like I was working at a comprehensive, general education high school. Lastly, he insinuated I was out on campus making waves and stirring discord among the staff by opening a discussion around the school's climate. After the principal showed his hand (metaphorically, of course), maybe I should have dropped it, or "Shut up and color," as a friend in the field would say. But I couldn't. The stakes were simply too high. Although I was a district neophyte, I felt there was no way I could set aside logical reasoning, dismiss my worldview, and "play the game of school." So, I openly challenged his claim.

I told the principal that the teachers were vigorously discussing the situation already, and they vehemently disagreed and opposed his philosophy and his fundamental approach to school discipline. He again laughed and stressed that it was the "nature of the beast." He then vowed to prove his point, and he did.

At the next staff meeting, he began by asking two questions: Is everything going well and are you satisfied with the school's policies and procedures? To my amazement, everyone in the room nodded in the affirmative to the first question. He then polled the group individually for an answer to the second question. He prefaced the polling with this comment, "Mr. Lockett seems to think all of you are having a problem with our policies and procedures." He then proceeded to query the staff individually, "Are you satisfied with the program?" One by one, they all answered in the affirmative, even a veteran teacher I felt would be open and honest about the situation. I couldn't believe it. I felt so stupid. After the initial wave passed, my next emotion was more sinister—fear. I was afraid we had arrived at a point where we were willing to sell our souls and the souls of our children for trinkets—a low paying job with mediocre benefits.

The next day, some of the staff avoided me like I had the plague; others stopped talking with me altogether. My friend and walking buddy, Al Collins, and Aziz Khalifa, a teacher and Black Muslim who was originally from Detroit, were the only teachers I can recall who continued an open and friendly dialogue with me. It was Al who tried to explain the nature of the education racket to me. He said they all knew what I was saying at the meeting was right and true, but it wasn't worth the opposition. He went on to say the only constant in schools was change. The people and programs changed with regularity, he said. He ended the dialogue by saying, "and this too shall pass." I told him he was probably right, but the students didn't have the luxury of waiting for the next round of nonsense. They needed an education now.

About mid-year, after I had put a student in check about his poor behavior in class, the principal called me into his office. Unceremoniously, he broke the news that I had no future at his school. "Mr. Lockett," he said, "At the end of the year you are being excessed." He went on to explain that meant I was leaving his school, but not fired altogether.

He told me that probationary or new teachers could be assigned a non-reelected status, which meant fired, without being provided a reason. He then said that because he "liked me," he had declared that my job was an "excess" or unneeded position for the next year. Just like that, I was not fired or banished from the district, but booted out of his school. I responded by thanking him and stressed there were no hard feelings. I then went on to reveal to him that I had already excessed his philosophy and leadership approach back when we had our initial ideology clash. Ironically, two or three years later, that principal was relieved of his position. I, on the other hand, would begin a journey that would take me to site teacher of the year, dean of students, assistant principal, principal, school change process creator and educational consultant. However, there were still miles on the educational road to be traversed.

... Alternative Learning for Behavior and Attitude (ALBA)

In 1999, I was hired by Principal Donald Mitchell. The school was called ALBA. In Spanish ALBA translates to new dawn or daybreak; in the SDUSD, it stood for Alternative Learning for Behavior and Attitude. It was the zero-tolerance, suspension, expulsion school for the district. I didn't know it at the time, but because of my mounting specialized experiences in education, and perhaps my law enforcement background, I was beginning to be pegged as an alternative education guy. To be candid about it, I didn't mind the pigeonholing at all. Alt-Ed was a perfect niche for me, or as Sir Kenneth Robinson, British author, speaker and international advisor on educational affairs would say, it was my "Element."[17] ALBA was the perfect match that almost didn't happen.

After being excessed, exorcised, or whatever, I was dropped into the district's bad teachers pool. The pool, and the process of selecting teachers from it, is sometimes referred to as "The Dance of the Lemons."[18] Once excessed and dumped into the lemon pool, it was the district's job to match me with a school that had a need. Because of my YOU experience, when I got the call from Don Mitchell about ALBA, I did a little homework. I asked the few friends that I had managed to keep about the assignment. Every single one of them told me that the place was a dangerous hellhole, and it was full of hooligans and rejects. I was advised that I should do everything in my power to avoid it. I took their dire warnings to heart. By interview day, I had amassed what I thought to be a foolproof failure strategy. Like the old O'Jays song, I came up with "992 Arguments" designed to ensure that I would not be hired.

Leading up to and during the interview, I employed all the "don't hire me" strategies in the book. I was late, and I didn't even bother to call. I wore dirty, wrinkled clothes. I hadn't washed my face, and I didn't brush my teeth. Near the end of the interview, because Don seemed to be signaling that he might look beyond the esthetics, I dropped what I thought to be my ultimate "botch the interview tactic" on him. They were my own little personal atomic bombs. I told him about my seedy and sordid ghetto background. I told him how, as a student, I had been the guy sitting in class with a stolen gun tucked in my waistband and concealed underneath my shirt. I went on to inform him how one day one of my brothers had borrowed it and shot two students on campus. I told him how I was sent to juvenile hall for carrying a knife at school after my gun had been confiscated. I even shared how I had broken into my high school on multiple occasions and had even arm robbed a few times. I finished him off by telling him about the time when I was twelve years old and had voted to kill a guy over a card game. (The incident resulted in my sister shooting the guy five times. Fortunately, he didn't die.) After hearing all that, Don hired me anyway. Two decades later, he and I still laugh about that interview. According to him, it was my so called atomic bombs that sealed the deal. He said he knew I could handle the situation. I ended up teaching at ALBA for four joyful years.

ALBA consisted of three sites—elementary, middle, and high school. My first assignment was at the newly formulated high school. It was a storefront on El Cajon Boulevard, smack-dab in the middle of an expanding Vietnamese business corridor with a thriving red-light district. Initially we had only two teachers and about 50 students. Just as in the boot camp, I taught Language Arts and History. As you might imagine, there were so many highlights from the experience that I can't possibly list them all. However, I will mention one because it was the one that, in my opinion, went the farthest towards setting our climate and solidifying us as a school community.

As a storefront, our building and my classroom had a floor to ceiling plate-glass window. When people walked by, if our blinds open they could see us and we them. I don't know quite how it all started, but at some point very early on, a little knucklehead started walking by and taunting our students. Eventually he became emboldened and began tagging our window with a marker. The first few times he did it, I did not see it occur. I learned of the vandalism only when the students began to giggle and whisper. By then, the tagger had disappeared into the bustling morning street traffic. I knew I had to respond as the giggles and whispers represented something more serious: non-allegiance. It meant the students had more loyalty to a clown on the street than to me and our school. The first thing I did was give them a pep-talk about what was really happening. I told them the guy was not only disrespecting me and our school, but by default, them. And he was doing it to their face. The talk apparently got their attention. After that, some of the students volunteered to remove the graffiti, and the next time the guy walked by, they ratted him out. Okay, they were good students who offered up the truth.

At the time of the incident, I happened to be in the reception area welcoming a new student. Suddenly, they all started yelling out that the tagger was at work. I believed them, and instead of walking back into the room and yelling at him through the window, I dashed for the front door. When he saw me exit the building, he dashed. I chased him down and across the street. I caught him in front of the McDonald's restaurant. I didn't catch him because I'm fast; I caught him because he was overweight and his pants were so saggy that I probably could have caught him if I had chosen to skip. I took him down and held him fast. Somewhere in the process, I noticed that he was not alone. As his buddy attempted to charge me, the cavalry showed up. It was not the police but two citizens—a Vietnam veteran, known in the area as Mr. Hawk, and a Lady of the Day, and probably night too. Mr. Hawk walked the street with a 5-gallon bucket and washed windows for a living. He and I had talked extensively about the Vietnam War, one of his and my favorite topics. The streetwalker and I had become waving and smiling friends after she had mistaken me for a client in our parking lot one morning.

As we stared down the tagger's buddy, the best thing possible occurred. Ms. Junker, our school counselor appeared beside me. She was not alone; accompanying her was a hoard of our students. With my full entourage staring him down, the guy decided to hightail it out of there. After the police arrived, searched the kid and discovered his crack pipe, which contained residue of prior usage, he was whisked away. I thanked my community partners, and we triumphantly returned to school.

Back inside, I asked Ms. Junker why she had decided to come to the location. Her response made me know that we were officially becoming a school community. She said she had attempted to keep our students in the building, but they insisted upon helping me. Being an astute educator herself, Ms. Junker pulled a page out of my playbook. Because they were determined to come to the scene, she decided to make it something of a supervised field trip. For the remainder of my time at ALBA, Mr. Hawk washed our windows free of charge, the working girl walked slowly past waving and smiling at us as we studied, several parents volunteered and periodically made special carne asada barbeque lunches, and we didn't have a single fight among our students. Ironically, as stated, that year I was voted ALBA Teacher of the Year. We had the makings of a great school.

At the end of my second year at ALBA, Don was promoted to principal of Gompers Secondary School, a large comprehensive site with approximately 1,700 students. The new principal assigned to ALBA was Jolie Pickett. Jolie had been assistant principal at YOU when I was there, so she already knew a fair bit about me and my philosophy. At the mid-year mark, she approached me and asked if I would consider a transfer to the middle school. According to her, it was not achieving its full potential. It was one of the greatest understatements ever made. I had heard about the shenanigans that were going on there, and I had visited the site after school and saw the property damage firsthand. The place was rabid.

The middle school was also in a storefront on El Cajon Blvd. It was little more than a block east of the high school. After going over and looking at the dynamics, I respectfully declined the offer. As a consolation, I proposed to go there at the beginning of the next school year. My rationale was simple. If I were to go into a less than inspiring climate, I wanted an opportunity to establish and set the posture from the start. The next year, when the middle school students arrived, we jumped on building and establishing the climate immediately. I told students we could not work in an environment that was not conducive to teaching and learning. After explaining what conducive meant, we got down to business. I stressed we had to clean the place up. Pointing up at the pencils stuck in the ceiling, then going to the graffiti riddled, filthy restroom, and finishing with the tagged-up desk and dirty, junky classrooms, I made it clear it all had to be corrected before we could begin school. A few of the carryover knuckleheads from the previous year balked. I was delighted.

In my opinion, the students who challenge your leadership are either vying for the position themselves or checking to see if you are really the leader so that they can relax. In an urban underserved school, I practically pray for leadership challenges. It's a true opportunity to win over the challengers. Furthermore, those who challenge are often actual leaders. They are usually just slightly misguided.

I gave the challengers an ultimatum. Of course, it was not in line with California Education Code, but I went for it. I told the students they could help with the cleanup or go home until we were done. Either way, it was me calling the shots. One or two students opted for home, and then a couple of copycats chimed in. Parents were called. After hearing my plan, all the parents told their students they would be staying and helping. Their challenge and my response was also a great parent contact setup.

Urban parents almost always get on board with positive initiatives that are explained to them in a respectful, authentic, colloquial vernacular. Thereafter, I also knew which parents I could call on for assistance with other school initiatives. So, with all hands on deck, I popped in a soul music cassette tape and we went to work.

Under my supervision, the students pulled pencils, painted walls, swept and picked up trash, washed the desks and mopped the floors. After the work was finished, I hung our rules and school posture. I didn't call it posture back then; it was just what we were about. I went to the district's Teacher Resource Center and made giant posters and banners that said things like: "Welcome to the fight of the century," "Intelligence versus Ignorance," and our only rule, RESPECT. The Class Rule graphic follows:

Then, every morning before we began the instruction, I gave a short inspirational warm up about the fight of the century to the entire school. It set the tone for the day. In a short time, the climate was set and the culture of learning activated. It was another great year.

At the end of the year, Don, who had his sight set on improving the school climate at Gompers, called and asked me if I would come and work with him for the next school year. I was having such a great time at ALBA, I declined the offer.

The following year, as a potential cost saving strategy, ALBA was moved out of the storefronts to a series of renovated small district campuses. I was reassigned to the larger high school. Even though the school more than doubled in size, it was another great year. Again, with too many highlights to list, I would be remiss if I didn't mention one.

During lunch, I always had an open-door policy. Thus, I always had a room filled with students. They ate their lunches, chatted, and watched television. To give them some space, and me a little mental relief, I usually sat at my desk and played chess on my computer. A few kids got wind of the chess action and started watching. Not surprisingly, some of them even knew the fundamentals of the game. Unfortunately, many had learned in juvenile hall. Of course, after watching me play, they were all sure that they could easily beat me. With all the trash talk flying about, I got a stroke of genius—start a Chess Club. Creating a Chess Club was not a new venture for me. While in Fresno, as a community volunteer project, I had organized and led a youth chess club. The club was in the recreation room at a high poverty apartment complex and consisted of elementary and middle school age kids. When I proposed the undertaking at ALBA, the administration was very open to the proposal and agreed to purchase a few tournament sets. We were off and running.

Initially it was a lunchtime activity, but it rapidly expanded to a full-fledged after school endeavor. The real hook came after I showed them the movie, *Searching for Bobby Fisher.*[19] Of course, they all believed themselves to be the next great one.

As the school year came to a close, I decided to give them a chance to test their skills. I sponsored the seven best players in the annual Balboa Park tournament at the San Diego Chess Club.[20]   Sadly, the next Bobby Fisher was not unearthed, but every ALBA player made it through the first round. They all had at least one victory, and one player, a Chaldean kid with limited English skills, made it all the way to the semifinal round. He had been sent to ALBA for taking a baseball bat to some students at his high school for taunting him. Those guys all attended summer school, mostly for the after-school chess, and they peacocked about and acted like intellectual jocks (regular students) all summer long.

While at a local mall that summer, I ran into Don Mitchell. After a bit of catching up, he once again asked if I would be willing to transfer to Gompers Secondary School for the upcoming year. When I inquired about the job, he said he wanted me to leave the classroom and become Dean of Students.

At the time, the Dean of Students position was new to the district, and even though I had been a teacher for four or five years, I didn't know what the job entailed. So, I asked. His response was classic Don Mitchell. "Well . . . I would like for you to come and look around, then tell me what you think you ought to be doing," he said. I agreed. The results of my walkthroughs, recommendations, and implementations eventually became the foundational principles of UE101.

... Samuel Gompers Secondary School

At Gompers Secondary, the 1700 students were spread throughout a combined two-campus mega complex. The campuses were joined by a paved blacktop road and several layers of fencing. I was told Gompers had at one point been a magnet school and the elaborate fencing system was used to separate the "wheat from the weeds." As a magnet, the theme had been science and technology, a forerunner of the STEM movement. According to the vice principal, the problem with the school was the constant feeling that days were spent keeping the bussed-in magnet kids (the wheat) separated from the buck-wild neighborhood kids (the weeds). By the time of my arrival, only the neighborhood students remained. Furthermore, I was informed that we were starting the year on heightened alert because of the way the previous year had ended. It seems that as the year came to a close, there had been a "riot" which stemmed from an incident between Black and Mexican students. The incident was described as so serious that motorcycle cops were required to patrol the campus while a police helicopter scouted from above.

After assessing the neighborhood and the school, which felt at least three times tamer than Mechanicsville and Carver high school, I offered my suggestions for improving the climate. After throwing in a few of his strategies and thoughts, Don accepted and approved the plan.

In four years of implementation, we posted some incredible results. Conflicts, violence, and suspensions were all substantially lower. According to Don, our suspension rate was reduced to about 5%, which was lower than the State average. In addition, there was not a single instance where the police had to be called in to restore order. While posting tremendous climatic gains, our academic gains (culture) were also outstanding. In the four years, our Academic Performance Index (API) (the measure to determine a school's academic performance at the time) increased by more than 60 points. Also, during that stretch, Newsweek twice listed us among the 1000 best schools in the country. It was during that period that I wrote my first book, *Urban Essentials 101: Unleashing the Academic Potential in Urban Underperforming Schools.*

About midway into our fourth year, Don called me into his office. He thanked me for contributing to what he termed four of his best years as a principal. He then insisted that I enroll in an administrative credentialing program at his expense. I took him up on it. Unfortunately, Gompers was closed at the end of that year. Our final staff meeting was incredibly sad. Several teachers and staff wept openly. Our students and many of the staff were eventually transferred to Lincoln High School, a complex nearly twice the size of Gompers Secondary. In the final analysis, Gompers became a charter middle school, and, just like that, it was over.

I was offered a transfer to Lincoln, but I opted for Samuel Morse High School. At the time, Morse, with approximately 2,500 students, was the largest school in the San Diego Unified School District. It was also known throughout the district as a behavioral nightmare.

After I interviewed with Morse's principal, he guaranteed me that I could use UE101 implementations to set our climate. With less than a full implementation, we achieved a 47% decrease in suspensions over the previous year. At the end of the school year, we conducted a teacher climate survey. In the survey, the overwhelming majority of the responses expressed a positive sentiment for the implementation. There was also a slight uptick in the school's API score.

Two years later, I accepted an assistant principal position at Keiller Leadership Academy (KLA), a San Diego Unified School District charter middle school.

... Keiller and Beyond

Keiller, nicknamed "Killer," was infamously recognized as a bad school. As a charter, it had broken away from the San Diego district with the hope of resolving its issues through self-determination. The principal, Joel Christman, was a man I held in very high esteem. Tertia Sartain, a capable leader in her own right, was assistant principal over academic affairs. I was hired as assistant principal of student affairs. The description and title for the two assistant principal positions— academic affairs and student affairs—fit perfectly into my belief about the inputs necessary for school achievement: inspiration and instruction.

Tertia and I had met at the University of San Diego as members of the same administrator's credentialing cohort in the Educational Leadership Development Academy (ELDA). During breaks, Tertia and I often shared our educational philosophy and vision. After hearing my take on urban underserved education and how I believed the UE101 process to be an answer to many of the challenges, she encouraged me to apply for the position at KLA.

I was very impressed with the hiring process that Keiller had developed. The application process was standard, Edjoin. Following the application process, however, there was a two-part interview. When the field narrowed to two or three candidates, we were asked to present our philosophy and plan to the entire staff. This should be standard practice for all administrative hiring. In my opinion, too many educational leaders seek a higher position without a coherent philosophy, vision and plan. The focus is then on resources rather than relationships. At KLA, however, they made it tough to get hired. You could not hide behind the rhetoric; you had to pony up a vision and a plan.

I delivered a PowerPoint presentation about the UE101 process and illustrated the implementations that I planned for KLA. I was so convinced UE101 was the way to go that at the end of my presentation I admonished the staff not to endorse me for the position if they were not willing to use the process. I was selected.

In one year, suspensions at KLA were reduced by 42%. A teacher sentiment survey yielded a 96% satisfaction rating, and academically we posted an 18-point increase in our API score. The next year, I left KLA for Orange Glen High School (OG). Without my presence as assistant principal, KLA's suspension rate remained steady, and the school's API increased by another 22 points. Stacey Roth, a KLA teacher during the implementation and later an administrator intern under me at Orange Glen High School (now principal there), provided a humorous, yet profound insight about the process. Referring to their higher API in my absence, Stacey joked that all they needed was the process. She went on to say that I was basically holding them back.

Leaving KLA for Orange Glen was a no brainer for me. Although I loved the KLA family, I could not turn down an opportunity to try the process in a demographically different district and at a large comprehensive high school. When I checked out OG's School Accountability Report Card (SARC)[21] data, I knew they were ripe and right for me. What I didn't know was whether they were ready for such a drastic course change. The divide proved to be about 50-50.

There were about 2,700 students at OG. The population was predominantly Hispanic, and overwhelmingly Mexican. The staff was even more homogeneous than the students. It was overwhelmingly white. However, as I doggedly articulated earlier, it's about relationship, race doesn't matter. Thomas Allison, an undoubtedly forward thinker, was the OG principal. When he hired me, I was the only black person in all the administrative offices. However, it never felt that way. The overwhelming majority of our adult relationships were good.

At the beginning of my first year, Tom tried hard to get the staff interested in the UE101 process. After some discussion, the case for change was just not strong enough, and no program modifications were made. I was disappointed and, quite frankly, I began contemplating a graceful exit strategy.

I completely believed that change, real change, was the catalyst for growth. I also believed and understood if all that changed were a few people here and there, you could almost certainly count on results remaining the same. This constitutes a mere first order change, akin to rearranging the deck chairs on the Titanic. For real and sustainable results, a second order change — a course or directional change — is necessary. At the end of the first year, our failure to change was rewarded with a 5-point decrease in our API score.

The next year, Principal Allison again expressed his desire to make a course change, and he pulled the trigger. At the beginning of the year, he gave me the go ahead to start training teachers in the process. During lunchtime meetings, I introduced about one-third of the staff to the practice. We established a non-traditional UE-styled In-school Suspension Classroom. This integral part of the change process will be discussed later. For technical reasons, however, involving opposition from the teachers' union regarding the staffing of the ISSC, it was eventually shut down. (As a point of reference, I agreed with the teachers. California Education Code clearly states the ISSC must be staffed "as otherwise provided by law," and that means by a regular teacher.) Nonetheless, even with the setbacks and partial implementations, at the end of year two, we posted a reduction in suspension days of over 300, and a 36-point increase in our API score.

The following year, I accepted a job as principal of Discovery High School, a continuation school in the Natomas Unified School District in Sacramento, California. There were two reasons for taking the job—the SARC, which indicated a heavy suspension toll on black and brown students and the prospect of full process implementation in a continuation school.

Discovery High School never had an enrollment of more than about 150 students and because of the campus chaos, some would say that was too many. During my tenure, the district advised of their desire to expand the school to 300. Of course, the expectation was to manage the growth with no additional staff and without an increase in suspensions and behavioral problems. Our student population reached only about 240, but our year was exceptional. We had just three on-campus fights all year compared to the previous year when they had reached double digits. By the end of the year, even with the substantial increase in enrollment, suspensions as a percentage of the population were dramatically down from the previous year.

My last year of work in schools was spent as principal at Valley Community School in Merced, California. VCS Merced is one of three Alternative Education Schools operated by the Merced County Office of Education. The other campuses were in Atwater and Los Banos, California. In 2011, after a districtwide process training, MCOE implemented the UE101 process in all three schools, under their school posture name, STRIVE (Safe, Trust, Respect, Inspiration, Vision and Encouragement). The first-year results were incredible. In schools known for violence, with up to 70% of the students at any given time on probation, the three schools together posted a 60% decrease in documented discipline related issues. The results were highlighted in a Merced Sun Star article by reporter Doane Yawger. The article was entitled *Conflict resolution for Merced, Atwater, and Los Banos students is working.*[23]

The process has since been adopted by the Merced Union High School District, Hanford Joint Union High School District, and other individual schools. So far, the results have been in line with the previously mentioned successes. For instance, in January 2015, MUHSD's Child Welfare, Attendance and Safety office published significant data pertaining to student behavior demographics. The data was reported to their School Board and indicated that behavior-related disciplinary issues were on a steady decline. The data included statistical comparisons over a three-year period for drug and alcohol entries; fighting, assaults and battery; home suspensions; dangerous students; truancy; and expulsion. Here is a snapshot of the results:

Drugs & Alcohol Entries	
2011-12 school year	366
2012-13 school year	300
2013-14 school year	324
2014-15 1st Semester	147

Fighting - Assault - Battery	
2011-12 school year	300
2012-13 school year	311
2013-14 school year	242
2014-15 1st Semester	68

Days of Home Suspension	
2011-12 school year	4284
2012-13 school year	3387
2013-14 school year	1951
2014-15 1st Semester	766

Dangerous Students	
2011-12 school year	1461
2012-13 school year	1244
2013-14 school year	1120
2014-15 1st Semester	245

Days of Truancy	
2011-12 school year	10,364
2012-13 school year	10,387
2013-14 school year	14,627
2014-15 1st Semester	*5,077

Number of Expulsions	
2011-12 school year	142
2012-13 school year	126
2013-14 school year	107
2014-15 1st Semester	51

This includes 1,577 unverified absences for the first semester

According to the Child Welfare, Attendance and Safety Office, the data "is a reflection of the many District efforts to create a more positive and respectful climate on our campuses." They go on to identify the implementations of change as "Restorative Justice, Character Counts, Anger Management Interventions, Drug and Alcohol program, Safe and Civil School implementation, the after-school ASSET's program and expansion of student clubs and activities, as well as increased diligence with common area supervision." As mentioned, Urban Essentials 101 was the exclusive purveyor of Restorative Justice for MUHSD

A CLEAR-CUT PATH TO CREATING YOUR PROCESS

After receiving and processing all the information to this point, several questions have likely arisen. Some questions might include: Why so much background information? What is the Urban Essentials 101 process? And, if the process really works, how do you go about implementing it? These and other questions about UE101 are answered throughout the remainder of this book.

> *A small body of determined spirits fired by an unquenchable faith in their mission can alter the course of history.*
> — Mahatma Gandhi

... Why So Much Information?

As demonstrated, I come from the urban educational trenches. I was a student, teacher, and administrator in urban underserved schools. My experiences have been in both alternative and general education settings. As such, I fully recognize that urban educators have encountered so many variations and versions of professional development strategies designed for school improvement that many have become justifiably skeptical. Therefore, as a countermeasure to this anxiety and skepticism, I believe it is necessary to do everything I can to distinguish our process from other implementations. One of the best ways to accomplish this is through experiential and historical transparency. I also recognize that, as the Mahatma Gandhi quote above suggests, a small group of fired up, dedicated folks, equipped with the proper knowledge and the right strategy, can change the world. Consequently, all the information provided to this point has been a part of my indoctrination and recruitment strategy. I am attempting to captivate and capture hearts. I am also attempting to fire up the spirits of urban educators to embrace a process that potentially can change the course of history for urban underserved students everywhere. So yes, I am actively recruiting you to become a believer in our philosophy and to make the UE101 process the mission for your school.

... What Do I Want You to Embrace?

I am endeavoring to get you to accept two fundamental ideologies—the principles of Restorative Justice in Schools and the Urban Essentials 101 method of delivery and implementation. So, let's examine these two principles.

... Restorative Justice in Schools and the UE101 Process

A few years ago, I read a thoughtful article written by Brenda Morrison, Peta Blood, and Margaret Thorsborne. The article was published by the Public Organization Review: A Global Journal. At the time of publication, Brenda Morrison, (Ph.D.) was a research fellow at the Centre for Restorative Justice at the Australian National University. Peta Blood was the Director of Circle Speak in New South Wales, Australia, and Margaret Thorsborne was the Director of Margaret Thorsborne and Associates, an international restorative practice consultancy in Australia, New Zealand, and the United Kingdom. The 20-plus page abstract was entitled Practicing Restorative Justice in School Communities: The Challenge of Culture Change. In the exposé, the trio laid out a series of stages and steps for implementing restorative justice in schools. After reviewing their work, I fully agreed with their presumptions and prescription. The graphic that follows illustrates the five stages of implementation as identified in the work of Morrison, Blood, and Thorsborne:

STAGES OF RJ IMPLEMENTATION IN SCHOOLS:	

Stage 1 : Gaining Commitment—Capturing Hearts and Minds	1. Making a case for a change
	  a. Identifying the need(the cost of current practice)
	  b. Identifying learning gaps
	  c. Challenging current practice
	  d. Debuking the myths around behavior management and what makes a difference
	  e. Linking to other priorities
	2. Establishing buy-in

Stage 2: Developing a Shared Vision—Knowing where we are going and Why	1. Inspiring a shared vision 2. Developing preferred outcomes aligned with the vision 3. Building a framework for pracrice 4. Developing a common language
Stage 3: Developing Responsive and Effective Practice—Changing how we do things	1. Developing a range of responses 2. Training, maintenance and support 3. Monitoring for quality standrads
Stage 4_ Developing a Whole School Approach—Putting it all together	1. Realingment of school policy with new pracrice 2. Managing the transition 3. Widening the lens
Approach—Putting it all together Stage 5: Professional Relationships—Walking the talk With each other	1. Promoting open, honest, tranparent and fair working relationships 2. Using restorative processes for managing staff grievance, performance management and conflict 3. Challenging practice and behavior-building integrity

As identified in the research of Morrison, Blood, and Thorsborne, there are five stages of execution recommended for the implementation of restorative justice in schools. The stages are as follows: Gaining Commitment, Developing a Shared Vision, Developing Responsive and Effective Practice, Developing a Whole School Approach, and Professional Relationships. Although written, codified and published in 2005, many of the goals, objectives, and strategies found in their implementation stages were already being realized and used by us in our work in San Diego, California as early as 2000. For instance, at Gompers Secondary, we simply knew it as our school change model. And we had gone a step further. Where the Morrison, Blood, and Thorsborne work had brilliantly identified the stages, we had proceeded to and succeeded in the practical application and implementation of the stages.

So, if you feel that everything I have been discussing to this point fits conveniently into stage 1 of the RJ implementation in schools—Gaining Commitment, Capturing Hearts and Minds—you would be correct. And the truth of the matter is this: if you cannot get urban educators to buy into the work of Morrison, Blood, and Thorsborne, it is going to be extremely difficult to convince them to use our process of delivery.

If you can accept the five stages of RJ in school, you are more than ready for an overview of UE101 implementation process. A graphic illustration of the UE101 process follows:

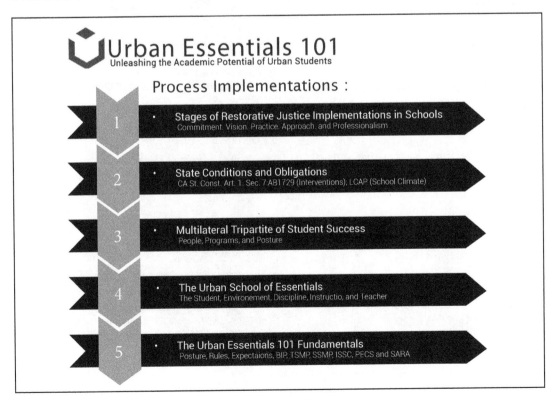

A full UE101 implementation in your school includes an understanding of the Stages of Restorative Justice in Schools; a review and understanding of some of the key State Conditions (laws) and Obligations surrounding Education Code and current proceedings and trends; and understanding of the integration of the Multilateral Tripartite of Student Success— people, programs and posture; an examination and understanding of the Urban School Essentials—the student, the environment, discipline, instruction and the teacher; and the development and implementation of the eight Urban Essentials 101 Fundamentals— school posture, rules, expectations, behavior intervention plan (BIP), teacher-student mediation (TSMP), student-student mediation (SSMP), in-school suspension classroom (ISSC), and problem effect cause solution (PECS) and survey analysis response and assessment (SARA).

The Morrison, Blood, and Thorsborne notion of the stages of RJ in Schools is a common thread throughout this book. Because their work is readily available and accessible online, I will not spend any more time elaborating on it. The remainder of our efforts will be spent on the direct discussion of the urban underserved dilemma and the UE101 process and its implementation as a solution. I do, however, encourage the reading on RJ in school communities.

THE ULTIMATE GOAL AND THE UE101 PROCESS AND IMPLEMENTATION

As stated earlier, the goal or aim of UE101 is to assist urban underserved schools in the development of a climate of safety while forging a culture of learning and achievement. This climate and culture arrangement is the fundamental assumption presumed to be the interconnected mechanisms for school achievement, and thus student success. There are five (5) fundamental factors which must be in place for student success to be achieved. The factors are Inspirational Leadership, Authentic Relationships, Proper Resource Alignment, Supportive Structures, and Quality Instruction. The graphic that follows illustrates the student success cycle.

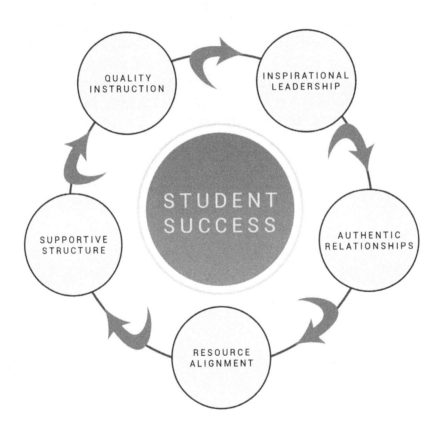

The best way to ensure that these components of the success cycle are implemented is through the development of an all-inclusive strategy built upon the foundational notion of maintaining a balance between a district or site's Relationships and Resources. Let's look at this relationship and resources dynamic

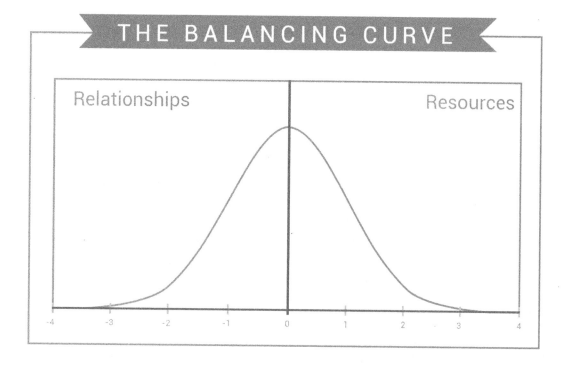

THE BALANCING CURVE

Relationships | Resources

It's all in how you arrange the thing... the careful balance of the design is the motion.
—Andrew Wyeth

... Relationships and Resources

The best indicator of a school's success lies in an examination of the calibration or balance of its relationships and available resources. It is through the relationships and resources that the climate and culture is established and sustained. Whether high performing or underserved, social dynamics are the principal driver, and they are always in a perpetual state of a balancing. This explains why a school can be a high performer for many years and as the social dynamics change, the level of achievement follows. This balance determines a school or district's level of achievement and success. Currently, in urban underserved schools, there is often an obvious imbalance, and the imbalance is mostly skewed towards the resources side of the equation.

As explained in my first book, *Urban Essentials 101: Unleashing the Academic Potential in Urban Underperforming Schools*, success comes down to these two variables—Relationships and Resources.   After over two decades of observing and implementing our process, I am more convinced than ever that this assumption is not only factual but imperative in understanding and rectifying underserved schools.   In other words, the relationships and resources must be implemented as part of a balanced approach to student success.   Furthermore, we must incorporate the understanding of these variables into the school environment as dependent entities. Currently in urban underserved schools, relationships and resources are generally viewed as independent variables. The fact of the matter is they are dependent upon each other if academic success is to be achieved. Simply stated, relationships and resources are needed together to build a climate and culture. Therefore, we must commit to the belief that relationships and resources must be present and properly balanced, as part of sustainable climate safety and culture of learning and achievement.

So why are we not balancing these variables? As alluded to in my previous book and early in this work as the "illegitimate legitimacy," the reason we rarely take a balanced approach in the education arena is that our policymakers do not historically come from the urban underserved environment. Therefore, the relationship component seldom warrants serious consideration. Relationships for many conventional educational framers are viewed as just another part of the communal landscape.

A clear view of this communal landscape idea is essential for understanding. Policymakers, with few exceptions, grow up where the relationship component is a given. The values of the home and the values of the school are, for the most part, relationally congruent. In fact, most research indicates that educational decision makers usually come from backgrounds that are closely aligned with one another. Thus, almost any teacher hired into the system fits into their concept and notion of what is a good teacher. However, this does not guarantee the teacher will fit well in the urban underserved school environment. Why is this? It is mainly because most of the hiring in school districts is done for and by individuals from high performing school experiences and perspectives. As a result, the politics and structures of urban education are geared towards the experiences of the elite. This experience differential could be called elitist bias.

Because of this elitist bias, programs inevitably end up being focused on instructional practices over relationship-building practices, and the resources follow. Unlike many have presupposed, I am convinced there is no conspiracy here. Instead of thinking about the phenomenon as white privilege, racial disparity, or social-class warfare, it should be viewed as a natural outcropping of the elitist altruistic spirit. It is not that different from the welfare debacle and other failed entitlement schemes—well intended yet marginally beneficial.

If educational framers could make the right decisions for the urban underserved, I'm convinced they would direct the financial resources towards the appropriate implementations and strategies to make our country the vanguard of the educational marketplace once again. There is no conspiracy. The U.S. educational leadership elite would close the achievement gap today if they knew how.

Furthermore, because the work of most watchdog and oversight groups tends to be viewed as an affront by the leadership, their response is often less transparency. This lack of transparency in turn creates greater mistrust, perpetuating the conflict. The recent social and political unrest, for example, appears to stem from the relationship, not resource, side of the model. In our society, money is spent like crazy, yet the socio-political outcomes are abysmal. When this occurs, as mentioned, people on both sides often do what seems to be a rational thing. They double down. Citizen protesters and politicians muscle up, and the opposition does the same. As it relates to schools, the logic is similar. From the perspective of educational leadership, low academic performance requires a materials upgrade or a resource investment, while urban underserved parents, teachers, and other affiliates are often focused on relationship inputs like safety. Our leaders appear to believe that we can spend our way out of the predicament. I think the Beatles said it best: *Money Can't Buy Me Love.*

Perhaps a more thorough or comprehensive investigation of the situation with a different set of experts would yield a slightly different result. However, the experts known within the circle tend to be those who are repeatedly called upon for solutions. A different set of experts would, perhaps, find that inspiration, encouragement, enthusiasm, and motivation—all relational inputs—are needed and not more math manipulatives, Chromebooks, or Smartboards. We must combine relationships and resources into one approach. The graphic that follows more fully explains what is meant by relationships and resources.

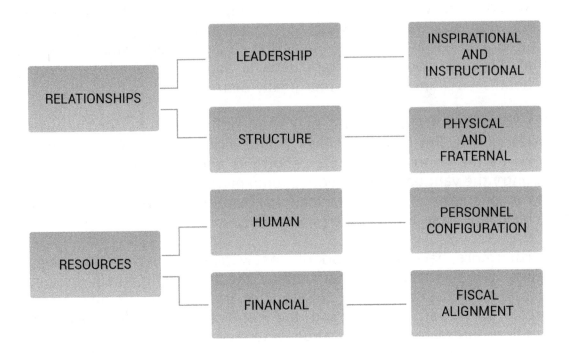

As you can see from the graphic, there are at least two types of relationships—leadership and structural. Leadership is described as recognizing everyone's potential and skills and building dynamic teams that bring together the best of these diverse talents.[24] Leadership in an underserved school setting is about having the ability and knowledge to encourage students to courageously become their best selves. It is about encouraging and guiding students along the pathway towards success. Therefore, leadership can be subdivided into two areas of application—inspirational and instructional. According to David C. Forman, chief learning officer for the Human Capital Institute and Friso van der Oord, global head of research for the Corporate Executive Board, there are "Eight Principles of Inspirational Leadership." The principles are as follows: inspirational leaders have the capacity to reframe, rethink, and outmaneuver others who attempt similar actions; they pursue significance; they live, share and scale the right values; they lead through culture; they earn and extend trust; they embrace transparency; they connect with others; and they collaborate across boundaries.[25]

At higher performing schools, you might be able to get away with being light on the inspirational side at the top of the organization. The principal, vice principal, teachers and even the superintendent in a high-performing district for that matter, may be able to produce continued high achievement without the benefit of inspirational leadership. The reason for this is there are so many other inspirational influences—parents, the clergy and other community enrichment organizations—that are readily available and at their disposal. In such an environment, the bulk of time may be spent on forging the culture of learning. This explains, in a succinct manner, how a heavy emphasis can be placed on instruction in those environments. We know the quality of instruction is the key ingredient in building student achievement. We also know a climate of safety precedes a culture of learning. It is inspiration not instruction that leads to safety.

A climate of safety has not been established on many of the urban underserved campuses that I have encountered. On quite a few of these campuses, because of a lack of consistent leadership at home and a dearth of supportive community structures, students often intertwine the teacher's inspirational leadership with the instruction. This is evident in the way many urban underserved students view instruction. It is not uncommon for underserved students to view their studies as an extension of the teacher. They often refer to instructional assignments as "their (meaning the teacher's) work," and will pick and choose which "teacher's work" they will do. This type of thinking should crystallize the significance of the need for inspirational leadership. It could be said that most underserved students are social-academic students, not academic-social. Student-athletes may be the ideal, but in urban underserved settings it is more likely to be athlete-students.

So, what about instructional leadership? It is also imperative. Teachers must know the course content. They must also be able to prepare students for rigorous testing and intergalactic, global competitiveness. (The intergalactic thing might be a bit too far.) However, knowing the content and/or instructional material and delivering it to its intended audience in a comprehensible manner requires a different and higher degree of skill. In urban underserved schools, it requires inspirational leadership. Inspirational and instructional skills are both parts of leadership and must be forged together.

The other type of relationship is structure. A structural relationship also has two forms—physical and fraternal. The physical relationship might include all aspects of the environment. They are the more concrete features. This can be as global as the community at large or as individual as a single classroom. The physical structures are usually the fixed apparatus—the buildings, furnishings, heating and air, the grounds, and even the quality of lunches. A classroom can be structurally arranged to advance or stifle relationships. The fraternal structure on the other hand, deals with one's interaction within the physical environment. It is how you define or characterize yourself within the physical structures. It is the answer to the question of what is your level of interaction in the environment. Are you afraid, creeped-out, gullible, standoffish, timid, unapproachable, and unfriendly, or are you approachable, dedicated, determined, friendly, honest, open, and stimulating? These fraternization traits in a nutshell are often what dictates and determines your relational success within urban underserved physical environments.

Now that you've got a handle on relationships, let's talk resources. Most people already understand the resource side of the model. It is usually just not labeled as such. Therefore, I'll be very brief. On the resource side of the model, there are two components—human and financial. The human side is obvious: it's the peeps (the people). In school districts, they are the individuals hired in one of three capacities— administrative, certificated, or classified. The financial resources are the actual dollars and how they are allocated to educate the students. To fully flesh out the graphic, the only other point I will make here is this: the personnel configuration (who are the people, where are they placed, and why?) and alignment of the financial capital (how is the money spent and why?) will ultimately determine the climate and culture of school sites, which in turn determines the level of success.

In many schools and districts, there is a tendency to point the blame in the direction of the teachers for low student achievement. Whenever I consult with a school or district, my stock response to that allegation is this: How can we blame the teachers when they don't select or hire themselves? I go on to explain that they don't fall from the sky like small meteors exploding onto campuses and wreaking havoc. They are selected through whatever human resources vetting process a district has established. So, before talking about how bad teachers are, a more genuine conversation should perhaps be centered on the resource side of the personnel configuration as it relates to the selection process. If the teacher selection process for urban underserved schools, and all schools for that matter, does not include a filtering system that sorts and selects for inspirational and instructional persons leaders, then that district is condemning itself to mediocrity and ultimately failure. The human resources selection process is vital.

As far as financial resources are concerned, the money is the money. And it is a finite resource. Therefore, it should go without saying that the way a school district spends its money is a direct reflection of its actual priorities. If a district, or school site, says they don't have funding for certain programming, what they are really saying is the implementation under discussion is not a priority, and not part of the current vision. Without hesitation, I say that I fully believe every district is entitled to set its own priorities. Therefore, in truth, all that really resides under the heading of human resources is personnel configuration. The agenda drives the money. The only question that remains is this, who are the people at the top?

When the relationship and resource model is activated, the bottom line goal should be obvious. The resources should be aligned to support the appropriately selected and distributed personnel to ensure the physical and fraternal structures are enacted and thriving as the leaders strive to inspire and instruct the students. With this information and reasoning, it is easy to see why the Relationship and Resource model is paramount.

THE CURRENT PREDICAMENT OR BREACH IN EDUCATION

Let's discuss some of the current trends. If the relationships and resources model as outlined in the graphic were more closely adhered to throughout the hiring process for urban underserved teachers and other staff, there would be no need for this book. However, because most districts do not use this, or a similar, model in the hiring process, issues often arise. In the hiring process, we often profess to be in search of the "best and the brightest" teachers available, but we consistently fall short. In many cases, at least during my tenure working in schools, districts indeed believed themselves to be hiring the brightest. In fact, for decades the average teacher scores on standardized test were among the highest among college students overall, but there has been a steady decline. According to data generated by Sean Corcoran, William Evans, and Robert Schwab, female teachers (who constitute roughly about 85 percent of teachers overall) were traditionally among the top 10 percent on high school standardized test scores. However, between 1971 and 2000, their testing achievement levels fell from 24 to 11 percent.[26]

An argument might be made that, in the past, we indeed filtered for the brightest, but were they the best? I think an accurate assessment of the brightest may be achievable via academic scholastic testing, but not so much when it comes to the best. The best is a more subjective measure therefore requiring greater specificity. Doctors or lawyers are probably bright people, but they are only the best when able to apply their academic and technical skills alongside their social skills. In the case of the doctor, it is called a "good bedside manner." "Best and brightest" in the school setting, therefore, should mean individuals with the skill and capacity to fully embrace, impart, and implement an effective balance of inspirational and instructional leadership with students. To my knowledge, there is no mechanism in place which directly accounts for or measures a teacher's capacity to build relationships. The "best and brightest" has by default come to mean only the academically "brightest," as measured by GPAs and standardized test scores. With no means or measures for identifying the best, measuring only for the academic brightest creates an illegitimate legitimacy for hiring.

In the next section, I will discuss an issue that occurs because of this imbalance. I refer to it as The Urban Underserved Breach. It is our number one dilemma in urban underserved schools and perhaps schools in general. The breach occurs when there is a stark mismatch between the teachers, staff, and students at a school site. Although the mismatch may come between the students and staff members at all levels, for this understanding, and the intense nature of their interaction, the focus will be on the mismatch with teachers. This breach is such a fundamental and prevalent issue that in my first book I created a graphic—the Teacher-Student Dissimilarity Graphic—to explain it. I think it is worth a short review and further elaboration.

A dissimilarity of pursuits dissolves friendship.

— Latin Proverb

Teacher – Student Dissimilarity Graphic

Urban Underperforming Schools	High-Performing Schools
←	→
Resources but **_no_** relationships	Resources **_and_** relationships
Teacher-student **_lack of_** familiarity Relationship deficient **Arrogance (false self-image and esteem)** Low buy-in, low standard performance *Domain of the Urban Student*	Teacher-student familiarity Relationship rich **Self-esteem** High buy-in, high performance *Domain of the Average Teacher*

A   M   Z

Let's examine the graphic. The dissimilarity graphic was designed to illustrate the relational difference between the average teacher and the typical urban underserved student. In underserved schools, many students don't learn, and they don't want to learn, from teachers they don't like. The usual definition of "like" is someone that they can't relate to. As we discussed earlier, many urban underserved students associate doing school assignments with how they feel about the teacher. Therefore similarity, or better said, a common understanding, is important. That's where the graphic comes in. It identifies the breach and its likely outcome.

The place to start this review is with the scale at the bottom of the graphic. The scale represents a continuum from A to Z. There are several ways to view the scale. The continuum could be used to illustrate the socio-economic, educational, or even the residential demographics of the people under examination. The demography really does not matter so much; the reality for this exercise is the same. There is a difference that exists. For our purposes, however, the continuum will represent social class.

The presumption in the graphic is that people, all people, come from a specific social stratification along a continuum of possible placements. Conveniently, the letter "M," happens to be the middle of the alphabet. On the continuum, it represents the middle-class stratification or median marker. Although this is a generalization, it could be said that the people who land on, or fall to the right of "M", as Ben Franklin might say, are more likely to be healthier, wealthier and, as measured by mainstream norms, wiser. It might be further stated that the pursuit of health, wealth, and wisdom constitute the relational commonalities and norms for their cohort. Conversely, the A through M group would share their own set of relational norms, localized and tailored specifically to their beliefs and values. With this line of reasoning in mind, it could be concluded that one's socioeconomic placement along the continuum will affect and determine their specific mindset. The beautiful thing about one's position and beliefs, at least in our country, is this: although the positions may often appear rigid, in reality they are not absolutely fixed. Our country provides a unique opportunity for upward and downward mobility.

It took me a long time to realize this simple principle surrounding mobility. Prior to my realization, because of the rigid appearance, I accepted the A-M belief system as being fixed. The adage, "a leopard can't change its spots," resonated with me. It was the localized gospel, and I believed it and all of the other established urban legends and myths. It wasn't until college that I could objectively look beyond the existing framework. When I began associating and interacting with M-Z students, regardless of their race, I began to understand the fluency within the continuum. The sooner this observation is made by urban underserved students the better. Without getting too far ahead of myself, I must make one important point. Teachers must understand that they may be the only access and introduction into the M-Z world for many of their underserved students. That makes them something of an ambassador. So just as with an ambassador, if they lack the relational skills needed to convey the message of mobility in an inspirational and encouraging way, the opportunity could be lost forever. When a student is not introduced to this reality early on, their progress could be encumbered for many years to come.

Although the concept of social capital has been around for almost a century, it only recently resurfaced as a mainstream convention. "Social capital" first appeared in a book published in 1916. It was presented as a term which described how neighbors could work together to oversee schools. In the book, author Lyda Hanifan referred to social capital as "those tangible assets [that] count for most in the daily lives of people:

namely goodwill, fellowship, sympathy, and social intercourse among the individuals and families who make up a social unit."

There were three main categories of social capital:

- Bonds: Links to people based on a sense of common identity ("people like us") – such as family, close friends and people who share our culture or ethnicity.
- Bridges: Links that stretch beyond a shared sense of identity, for example to distant friends, colleagues and associates.
- Linkages: Links to people or groups further up or lower down the social ladder.[27]

The ability of teachers to be available as bridges and links through inspiration and instruction is crucial. Teachers may be the only social capital in the lives of many urban underserved students. Research indicates that teachers may be deficient in this area.

All of the available research indicates that teachers by and large come from the M–Z domain. Conversely, most urban underserved students are from the A–M region. If this data is accurate, it would stand to reason that most teachers would likely be ineffective when it comes to interacting, inspiring, and instructing students from the A–M demographic region. Using this logic, it would also stand to reason that teachers who are highly effective in the M–Z region would become less effective as they moved across or down the scale towards A–M. I refer to this scale as the Relationship Effectiveness Continuum. With this understanding, it should be easy to comprehend the notion of the existence of a relational barrier or wall along the continuum. The concept of the Relationship Effectiveness Continuum and the relational wall is graphically illustrated.

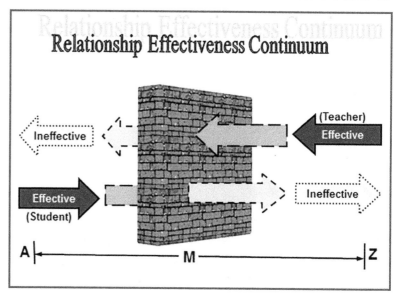

Teachers who must cross the divide, try though they might, often find themselves relationally hitting the wall and becoming less effective academically and socially. It becomes almost the same as attempting to teach in a foreign country without the luxury of knowing, speaking, and understanding the nuance of the local language. In other words, it's like having three process exchanges taking place instead of two. Instead of the teacher providing the content and the students receiving the content, an intermediate step exists—the translation of the original language that you don't quite understand, then making it meaningful in the context of the new instruction.

But this isn't a one-way street; it goes both ways. For students who encounter M–Z teachers, the exact same dynamic and divide exists. The best example I can provide of this phenomenon comes from my own experience in college. In my first class, the professor sounded so eloquent. The only problem was, because of my urban underserved background, I didn't have a clue about what he was trying to convey. He was speaking English, but at certain junctures, he may as well have been speaking Mandarin. His academic vocabulary was so high that at times it really sounded like a foreign language. I would understand a sentence or two and then a language anomaly would pop up. I would then try to adjust by deciphering the anomaly and reconstructing and reconciling the meaning in context. As I deciphered, the professor continued full steam ahead. In the end, I got some of the lecture but not really enough to put it together into a meaningful whole. I would literally feel lost in translation. Therefore, my focus was only partially on the content being delivered, as I was busy trying to decode the individual words. Under normal circumstances, a two-step process would transpire: the professor provides the information and the student receives it. In my case, there was clearly a three-step process: the professor provides the information and I receive some of it; then the deciphering and reconciliation process commences. And this was only the academic processing; socio-emotionally I was a wreck.

Because of all of the academic anomalies, fits and starts, I would sit there and privately question myself about my own intelligence and whether I measured up. Although I eventually learned to compensate, the actual remedy should not have been mine. It would have been more beneficial to me if the professor had introduced the terms for M–Z and then rephrased it for A–M comprehension. The reason it wasn't done that way is probably because it wasn't in his repertoire. I was in college and the level of academic comprehension was expected to be higher. However, I have seen the same phenomenon playing out on a daily basis in urban underserved schools.

Due to current hiring dynamics, the likelihood is that the exact same outcome will continue to persist. When M–Z teachers are placed in A–M schools without proper preparation, both teacher and student become weaker. And because there is such a dearth of A–M experienced teachers available in urban underserved schools, a peculiar phenomenon often occurs. Students begin to identify with and respect one another along with a host of other dubious personalities as their primary role models and leaders. Teachers are then relegated to something far less than their traditional esteem. By the way, although I will not go very deeply into the thinking, this would also be my chief rationale for not supporting School Choice or the arbitrary transferring of veteran teachers from M–Z to A–M schools. All that usually happens in those cases is a reverse relationship effectiveness continuum, not to mention the brain drain in both directions. Further, it also negatively affects other organizations like the Parent-Teacher Organizations (PTO) and School Site Councils (SSC) as the parents of the outsourced students are frequently the same people. This breach is also the technical definition of conflict—a mental struggle derived from incompatible or opposing goals and wishes.[28]

To continue with the dissimilarity graphic narrative, beyond the A–Z social class dynamic are the characteristics of the two distinct school domains—urban underperforming/underserved and high-performing schools. The urban underperforming/underserved school domains (A–M) and high-performing school domains (M–Z) have a set of their own individualized characteristics. In high-performing school environments, one often sees a harmonious balance between the relationships and resources. Furthermore, because of their similarities, teachers and students appear and respond to one another in a more familiar and less conflicting manner. As a result of this familiarity, the environment becomes more relationship rich. In a relationship-rich environment, real self-esteem flourishes. When self-esteem is present and flourishing, there is usually high student buy-in, leading to a higher standard of performance. On the other hand, in urban underperforming / underserved environments there is a near opposite effect. Although of late, resources have been in abundance, it has not been the same for relationships. Because of this lack of relationship, teachers and students suffer from a lack of familiarity resulting in a relationship deficit. When a relationship deficit occurs, arrogance or false self-esteem among the students usually emerges. The result of this development is low student buy-in. Low buy-in, of course, results in a low standard of performance.

The importance of this balance between relationships and resources was brought to bear in a 2012 study by the Program for International Student Assessment (PISA). PISA is an association that was formed under the Organization for Economic Cooperation and Development (OECD). PISA compares test scores of 15-year-olds from more than 65 developed countries in math, science, and reading. At the time of this particular study, we (the USA) ranked somewhere around 36th among all of the nations tested. The majority of the other countries, including Shanghai-China, the top ranking country, performed better while employing far fewer fiscal resource inputs, including technology in the classroom.[29] Although we tout the use of resource inputs such as technology as a significant factor for student success, when considering the results of the PISA research, I would have to conclude that while technology in the classroom may be admirable and desirable, it is probably not a major factor in student achievement.

When trying to decipher the reason for the low USA performance and conversely the high Chinese performance, educators seem to think that the problem derives from two sources—a lack of discipline and the need for more highly trained teachers. The consensus was that the disciplined approach to education helped explain Shanghai's success.[30] I believe, however, that it goes a little deeper. I believe it is more about inspirational relationships. In fact, the PISA report stated that as a result of the relationships, students in China are more likely to be happier at school, leading to higher achievement. The PISA graphic that follows illustrates a correlation between happiness at school and correspondingly high math achievement. From the graphic, it is easy to see that Shanghai, Macao and Taipei all scored in the top quartile for happiness at school and high achievement.

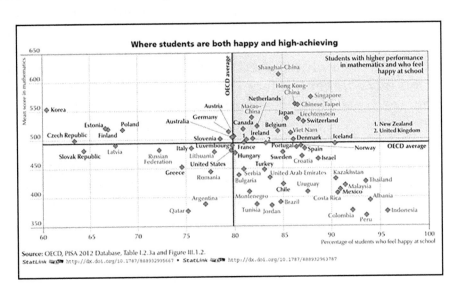

The correlation results were also consistent when examining US schools. The 2013 PISA report succinctly spelled out the findings. Here is what the report had to say about successful schools in the US: Schools in the United States with better than average performance tend to have more positive student-teacher relationships, even after accounting for the socio-economic status and demographic background of students and schools and various other school characteristics.[31] It is really all about the relationships. Judging by past decisions, however, it is possible that we could ignore these findings. If we do take heed, I can only hope and pray our response to this report won't be good bye Smart Board and hello Chromebooks and Apple TV. Instead, I hope that we will implement a balanced approach that allows us to keep the technology and boost the inspirational relationship building efforts as well.

If we look at most failing urban underserved schools and compare them with their higher performing counterparts, some separated by only five or ten miles in distance, it is easy to see that the high performers have both—relationships and resources—intact and working for them. Students who attend the high-performing schools are generally happier. They have more stable and appropriate school relationships, and they are often more involved in community and school activities. Their parents are more inclined, and sometimes better financially able, to support their schools. They (the students and their parents) typically identify with and support their teachers on a multitude of levels—socially, educationally, financially, and, in many cases, even religiously. In short, they have an abundance of social capital. However, it all starts with their relationships being intact. Relationships and resources working together make all the difference. The only question really remains is, what do we do now?

WHAT DO WE DO NOW ?

A Clear-Cut Pathway to a Climate of Safety and a Culture of Learning and Achievement

... What do we do now ?

So, what do we do now? In short, we change. And it must be a second order change—a qualitative and quantitative systems change. We must first change our attitudes and then our actions. This is usually the point in a book, lecture, or professional development where the writer and/or presenter ends the exploration, thanks the audience, closes up shop, and makes a speedy exit. It is also the point where veteran educators begin to suspect they have just been complicit in another PD flimflam. It is the time when it starts to feel that there was plenty of cloud formation, but little or no rain. Fortunately, we are about to change that dynamic. You are about to be provided with foundational principles, structures, and implementations for effecting positive change in your urban underserved schools. In short, we are about to move from beyond the cloud cover to measurable precipitation.

... The Tripartite of Student Success—People, Programs, and Posture

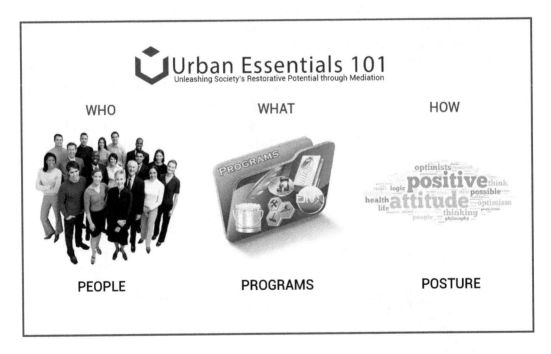

As stated, the key to building a climate of safety, which inevitably leads to a culture of learning and achievement, is through the balancing of a school site's relationships and available resources. This relationships and resources balance is realized through the positive development and deployment of a school site's People, Programs, and Posture.

At UE 101, we commonly refer to this people, programs, and posture change model as the Tripartite of Student Success. This people, programs, and posture model is a guide for establishing the Who, What, and How for the process. In other words, it lays a clear pathway of understanding of who will be doing the work, what the work will entail, and how the work is to be done. So, with the relationships and resources balancing act in mind, and the people, programs, and posture model as guiding principle for the who, what and how of the implementation, we will now begin the task of outlining our process.

... An Examination of the 3P's

The entire success question in urban underserved schools comes down to the development, implementation, and sustainability of the 3Ps. When they are properly established and nurtured, schools realize the results in several ways. The improvements may be summed up under the umbrella of greater campus pride. This is measured by elements such as an increase in general respect and more positive interactions between teachers and students. The manifestation of its presence can be seen through behaviors such as less graffiti, profanity, vandalism, violence, and even less aimless wandering about on campus. There will also be a lower rate of suspensions and higher average daily attendance. There should also be greater teacher satisfaction and retention, and, of course, higher standardized test scores. In short, when a thoughtful approach is taken to the selection, preparation, and deployment of the 3Ps, a climate and culture that is conducive to teaching and learning will emerge. So, let's probe a little deeper.

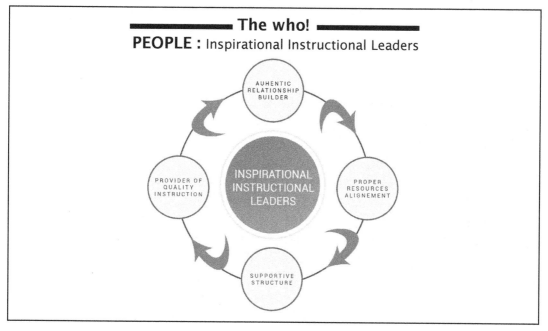

• **The People**

In urban underserved schools, a vigorous argument could be made that the people (the school staff) are the single most significant element and indicator of student success. Therefore, it stands to reason they must be carefully chosen, developed, nurtured and supported. Horace Mann, who is considered by many to be the father of public education, acutely understood the importance of this ingredient. It is this understanding which led him to launch the Common School Movement.[32] Mann's vision was to train and anchor schools with teachers who were taught using a common set of rules and values. The goal was to have teachers with the ability and capacity to provide students with uniform instruction in "words and moral teachings." It is these words or instruction and moral teachings or inspiration that led me to the conclusion that teachers must possess two essential abilities: they must be able to inspire and instruct students.

I call those teachers, and any other school affiliates for that matter who can do this, Inspirational-Instructional Leaders. Who are these leaders and what are the attributes and traits necessary to be one? It should come as no surprise that they are the people who possess the characteristics necessary to instill the "words and moral teachings" identified by Horace Mann. They are the teachers who can implement and transfer these structures to their students. The traits needed for inspirational instructional leadership are as follows:

* The capacity to develop authentic relationships with students and staff
* The ability to properly align the resources at their disposal
* The capacity to build or erect the needed supportive structures
* The ability and capacity to provide a level of high quality instruction

Earlier, we established the eight principles of inspirational leadership: 1. Rethink and reframe or the ability to be nimble and ready to adapt; 2. Pursue significance or be prepared to explain what you are teaching and why it is important; 3. Live, share, and scale the right values or Mann's moral teachings and/or stage 5 of RJ in schools: Professional Relations, which is walking the talk with each other; 4. Lead through culture or intentionally shaping meaningfulness, beliefs, customs, and perceptions; 5. Earn and extend trust; 6. Embrace transparency; 7. Connect with others; and 8. Collaborate across boundaries.

To be this inspirational instructional leader, it is necessary to demonstrate and apply these principles through the implementation components for student success. Therefore, an inspirational instructional leader must use these principles to build authentic relationships, properly align the resources at their disposal, build the necessary supportive structures, and provide rigorous quality instruction. Now that we have a working knowledge of the needed abilities, characteristics and traits, I will spend a little time fleshing out the components.

The inspirational instructional leader must be able to build authentic relationships. If the desire is to build and maintain authentic relationships, a definition might be in order. What is the definition of an authentic relationship? An authentic relationship is an association that is believed to be genuine and real. It is assumed to be worthy of acceptance on its face value and should project a true reflection of one's character, personality, and spirit. With this as our working definition, it should go without saying that an authentic relationship must be positive.

After several years of research geared towards assigning a set of components for creating and sustaining authentic relationships, I settled on six. The principles that were chosen for establishing and maintaining an authentic relationship are as follows: be ready to extend trust, have open and honest communication, be tolerant of individual differences, have high expectations and standards for interaction, and be ready to extend and practice forgiveness. All the great inspirational leaders I have ever known possessed and practiced these traits. I could easily have used 1 Corinthians 13:4-7 for our definition—be patient and kind; don't be envious, boastful and proud; don't dishonor others; don't be self-seeking or easily angered; don't keep records of wrongs; and don't delight in evil but rejoice with the truth; always protect, always trust and hope and preserve—but I did not want to scare anyone away. The point is this: the first step towards becoming an inspirational instructional leader is to build authentic relationships. The next step is proper resource alignment.

Proper resource alignment is important. All teachers have a set of resources that have been assigned and are at their disposal, and they should maximize their deployment. For greatest effectiveness, those resources must be seriously assessed and properly operationalized. The resources on a macro-level include the people, programs, and posture. On a micro-level, they will include everything from books and materials to teaching strategies and technology. They also include the physical and fraternal environment, including the classroom structure, right down to the cafeteria worker and the custodian. And I cannot stress enough the importance of including other affiliates such as the principal, counselors and all other classified staff. Further, parents and other community members should also be properly aligned and maximized. The way a teacher allocates and employs these resources will, to a great degree, determine the overall climate and culture not only on campus but in each individual classroom.

The next component that must be activated and employed by the inspirational instructional leader is the building of supportive structures. This directly links to the capacity to build authentic relationships and properly align your resources. Supportive structures are the actual implementations designed to assist the teacher in the teaching process and the student in learning process. Think of it as universal scaffolding. Supportive structures may be climate or culture based. A great example of a climate based supportive structure is school breakfast and lunch. They can be as benign as proper lighting and visibility on dark mornings or as elaborate as a warm early morning arrival room complete with a hot chocolate stand. It is preferable that this morning hot chocolate lounge be staffed by a teacher. It is a great venue to meet and build relationships with a wide range of students. Climate based supportive structures might also include an in-school suspension classroom, an afterschool tutoring program, or even a morning and after school parent escort program—a structure that allows groups of parents to walk along with students to and from school. At Keiller Leadership Academy, we even used parents as morning and after school parking lot traffic monitors. Our city police trained the parents on proper parking lot etiquette and safety. This turned out to be a great way to get a dialogue going between parents and their community police, as well. Other more fixed climate based structures might include clear and simple school rules and expectations, and even lunchtime kiosks for maintaining orderly lines and reinforcing appropriate wait skills.

Culture based supportive structures are designed to support fraternized relationship building. They might include rites of passage, rituals, and classroom and campus jobs. Things like uniform greetings, standards, handshakes at the door and interacting with students on the playgrounds, at lunch, and even school sponsored events and activities.

Some supportive structures, like the early morning arrival room with hot chocolate mentioned earlier, would fit into the category of both climate and culture based. It would provide a safe and warm (climate based) place for students to wait for classes to begin, while also serving as a great place for teachers to drop by, sip a cup of chocolate and build relationships (culture based) with students. Another good example of supportive structure is the open-door policy.

As mentioned, I would allow students to bring their lunch and eat in my classroom. They could watch TV, use their electronics, and even play chess against me. It was during my open-door lunch policy that I received much of my instruction in Tagalog, the native language of the Philippines. It provided students a climate of safety and me an opportunity to build relationships and reinforce our school culture. The room would be packed. I also had an open-door policy as vice-principal and principal. I simply scheduled nothing at the end of the day and waited. Teachers and students would drop by. If I wasn't there, they just made themselves at home and waited. Some students played video games on their phones; a few teachers graded papers while we chatted. Supportive structures may also include assignment rubrics, reading logs, course outlines and graphics, and other instructional manipulatives and strategies. Technology is also a supportive structure. (A note on technology: Make technology in the classroom, and possibly on campus, a student job. It gives them responsibility, which leads to greater buy-in. Not to mention, they are usually more tech savvy.) They might include mechanisms and contraptions such as emails, tweets, blogs, gradebook programs and other interactive communication sources. My only advice here would be, just don't allow them to become the replacement for face to face interaction. Supportive structures may be individualized and classroom specific. For maximum effectiveness, they ought to be school and even district wide. Again, try to think of them in the same manner as the scaffolding process. They are all the environmental constructions designed to bring about a better relational understanding and to facilitate teaching and learning.

When authentic relationships are recognized, the available resources properly allocated and aligned, and the supportive structures for reinforcing learning are established, all that remains is the implementation of high quality instruction.

I must begin this discussion with another confession. If I have a weakness in my repertoire, it is in rigorous high quality instruction. There is a slight chance that I may not be as bad as I think, but when compared to some of the other more skillful Brainiacs I have encountered, I must consider myself a quality instruction lightweight. However, because of the implementation of the other components, the students I taught usually excelled among their peers. On some level I am glad I was not better materially prepared. I believe it was my instructionally lightweight status that caused me to maximize relationships, resource alignment, and structure building.

I would like to make it clear that I am not proposing nor supporting lower standards for quality instruction. In fact, I believe the level of instructional rigor should be higher. I will only say that to achieve a high level of quality instruction in urban underserved schools, the other components must be present and in place as well.

Because of my lightweight status as it relates to instruction and the fact I realize most teachers are content ready, I will not spend a significant amount of time elaborating on quality instruction. Another reason for not investing a great deal of time and effort on quality instruction is this: Over the past two decades, I have attended numerous high quality professional developments in this arena. The facilitators typically do a great job, and the teachers usually learn the material and go back and attempt to implement it. Therefore, in urban underserved schools, I do not view the availability of high quality instructors as a huge problem. The problem, as far as I can see, appears to be in receiving the teaching time to deliver the lesson and the proper respect from the audience (the students) to receive it. So, now, I will only reiterate that quality instruction is vital as well. It is the programs run at a school site, however, that determine the lesson delivery time and the respect and responsiveness of the students. So, now let's tackle the area of programming.

- The Programs

━━━━━ **The what!** ━━━━━
PROGRAMS : A Climate/Culture Approach

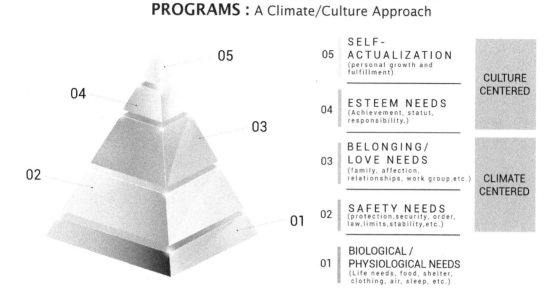

Over time, Inspirational Instructional Leaders become instrumental in the development and implementation of the site's programs. The programs are the "what" you do at your site. They are the approaches and methodologies used in creating and sustaining a cohesive and consistent school climate and culture. Programs include all the educational, operational, and training practices and systems deployed. Therefore, every program implemented at an urban underserved school, or any school for that matter, should draw its impetus from one of the categories discussed here. Furthermore, to ensure a greater opportunity for effectiveness, they should not only be educational, operational, and training based, but they should also be guided by a proven operational philosophy. I believe the operational philosophy that schools should be guided by is Abraham Maslow's Hierarchy of Needs.[33]

Most educators recognize and accept Maslow's hierarchy. In a room full of educators, one would be hard-pressed to find a single person who is not familiar with his pyramid. We know that it is directional and tiered, and we also know there are five steps or stages. What we sometimes do not seem to recognize is the fact there is a divisional assumption inherently built into the model. The assumption is that the steps can be subdivided into two categories. In other words, the hierarchy is not only structured in a step-by-step directional, tiered, and ascending order; it also has an overlapping or co-mingling quality. It is this two-part division and its overlapping nature that is my contribution to Maslow's work.

The pyramid can be subdivided into regions corresponding with climate and culture. In the climate-centered portion of the hierarchy, we find bio-physical, safety and, in an overlapping or co-mingled manner, love, belonging and relationship needs. In the culture-centered region of the hierarchy, we also find love, belonging and relationship needs. Relationships, therefore, are both a climate and culture element. Then we continue up the cultural ladder to the esteem and self-actualization needs. Staying with the ladder or hierarchy theme, it is logical to conclude that the higher one climbs, the greater and more diverse the set of skills required. In other words, each rung or step on the needs hierarchy requires a different set of skills to facilitate achievement. The skills necessary to make a campus safe are somewhat different from the set needed to effectively build relationships, enhance esteem, and deliver content.

Here is another way to think about it. Most people possess the skill level necessary to wash windows at their home. However, to wash windows on a skyscraper would be a different ballgame. In both scenarios, windows are being washed, but washing windows on a skyscraper requires a more in-depth set of skills and understanding. I would say this is the difference between working in an A–M and an M–Z school.

From the previous examples and the illustration in the program climate and culture graphic, one can easily discern that the belonging, love, and relationship needs area appears to be something of a logical divide that blends the two areas into one fluid system. In society and, as a microcosm of society by default, schools, we must recognize that the ingredients required for building successful communities are the same elements required for building successful schools.

We must also accept that each hierarchical level builds upon the previous one. In essence, as my need for food, shelter, and clothing diminishes, my desire for safety increases. I know that I must be the crown prince of weird examples, but this one will crystallize my point. An armed robber, burglar and even a prostitute will sacrifice their safety in exchange for fulfilling their physical needs. White flight, at least in my opinion, is as much about presumed safety as racism. Then, as I begin to feel safer, my desire for appropriate, fully integrated relationships increases.
It is at this relationship juncture that the switch from climate to culture begins. As positive relationships increase, the desire for esteem and achievement, both academically and socially, increases as well. The full manifestation of culture has now begun to emerge. When all the prerequisite hurdles have been cleared, a person (and students qualify

for this category), community, city, or a complete society becomes firmly established and self-actualization begins to emerge. Why do we need self-actualization? It is because this is where altruism—or doing a thing because it's the right thing to do—resides. It is the state where the utilitarianism principle of "the greatest good for the greatest number" dwells.[34]

When, or if, we reach the level of self-actualization in school, not by all but by a concentrated and significant mass, the environment becomes wholly conducive to teaching and learning. In the urban underserved education model of today, we are attempting to forge the notion of a culture of learning without first establishing a climate of safety. Currently, we do a good job in the biophysical realm. However, there is much room for improvement in the other domains. It appears we want achievement and actualization without first securing safety and relationships. I do not think this can be done.

So why did I elaborate on all that crap about Maslow's hierarchy and its climate and culture division? Well, it's all about an invitation to change. I am an advocate for a climate and culture approach and focus in schools. Amazingly, I do not think most schools and districts are averse to changing; I believe the issue is really about and knowledge to facilitate the change.

Regardless of the program, whether it is relationship or resource based, a restorative justice initiative or the purchasing of math manipulatives, the motivational and operational question should be the same. Where does the implementation fit into Maslow's hierarchy? When using a pyramid-based, climate and culture centered, balanced programming approach for site transformation, the most significant operational feature should then become the development of a school posture, or how we treat one another on the journey to student success.

- The School Posture

━━The How!━━
SCHOOL POSTURE

FAIRNESS
ACCOUNTABILITY
INTEGRITY
TRUST
HONESTY

The school posture is the de facto mission. It is the school's guiding principle. It, therefore, should be the very first operational component to be developed at your site. Your school posture is the one thing all affiliates—teachers, students, staff, parents, and other community members—should know, understand, and buy into. The school posture expresses what you all believe and how everyone behaves and agrees to interact with one another.

In the best-case scenario, your school posture should express all the hopes and desires of the school's mission. It should be far superior and treated with more deference than the school's mascot and other symbols and amulets. Webster's dictionary defines posture as the position or bearing of the body whether characteristic or assumed for a special purpose; [it is] a conscious mental or outward behavioral attitude.[35] As Webster's definition implies, it's the conscious, mental attitude assumed for a special purpose. In the case of urban underserved schools, it should be for the purposes of climate stabilization, furtherance of the culture, and assurance of academic achievement.

School posture is not a new thing. Every school already possesses a posture. It may not be written or posted, but it is usually understood. Whether poor or prosperous, a posture is always present. The only questions that emerge are: who is setting it and for what purpose? Whether or not we want to admit it, many of us have worked at or visited a school site where the posture was being set by the wrong group. Whether it was gang members, athletes, a small contingency of primadonna staff members, or a handful of marauding parents, the posture was clear. If we had to reduce those postures to one word, it would be FEAR (Frustrating, Egotistical, Arrogant and Rude).

In some schools I have visited, the posture of fear was so clearly established it was almost palatable. It goes without saying that a school's posture could be positive or negative. For example, if gang members are setting and controlling your school posture, the climate will most likely feel tense and unsafe, producing a negative culture. Conversely, if an inspiration and instruction-based school site leadership team establishes and sets the posture, it is more likely to feel safe and productive. So, it is not only important but imperative that the posture is immediately instituted and intentionally established by the appropriate affiliate group.

A posture should be a single word. Hopefully that one word is not FEAR. The word should also constitute an acronym that embodies the desired outcome for the school site. If I found myself working on a campus that did not have a collaboratively developed, staff-driven posture, I immediately began the process of developing one. While working as Dean of Students at Gompers Secondary School in San Diego, I deliberately set out to develop a school posture. After many hours of impromptu discussion, pondering, and research, I came up with the word FAITH. FAITH stands for Fairness, Accountability, Integrity, Trust and Honesty. Thereafter, it was my absolute commitment to engage and interact with the staff, students, parents and other affiliates from this posture. If a school accepted the posture of FAITH, we then set out to make it the preeminent directive, surpassing the mascot and fulfilling the mission. And, if the FAITH posture was not accepted, we would immediately begin the process of collaboratively creating a shared one.

The school posture should be prominently displayed, not just as a single poster affixed to a wall somewhere, but as systematic, strategically placed items that are reinforced daily. It should be that one thing that encompasses, emphasizes, and supports the ideals and standards of five stages of restorative justice in schools that we discussed earlier. Your school posture should be the platform for gaining a commitment— capturing the hearts and minds of all affiliates; developing of a shared vision; developing a responsive and effective practice; fostering a whole school approach; and building and establishing professional relationships. Let's look at a few school postures.

The following selections illustrate examples of postures adopted and implemented by schools in California:

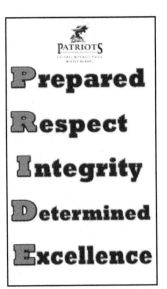

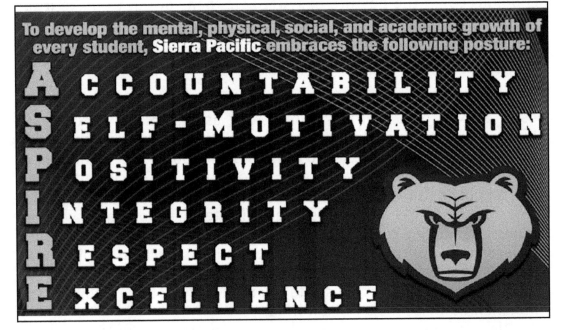

POSTURE
IMPLEMENTATION:

PRIDE!

Productive
Be punctual
Be prepared
Work towards goals
Respect
Be courteous and kind
Use appropriate language
Dress for success
Integrity
Always be honest
Model good character
Be accountable for person actions
Determination
Work hard everyday
Request help if needed
Be positive and encourage others
Equality
Be fair
Create a safe environment for all
Accept others' differences

The importance of developing and implementing a school posture is obvious. It is the unifying touchstone. As mentioned, it is and should be the first structure that is advanced and established at your school site. A strong posture ensures buy-in. Without a doubt, the proper establishment and implementation of a school posture will set the tone for a positive school climate and culture.

THE EIGHT FUNDAMENTAL UE101 PROGRAM IMPLEMENTATIONS

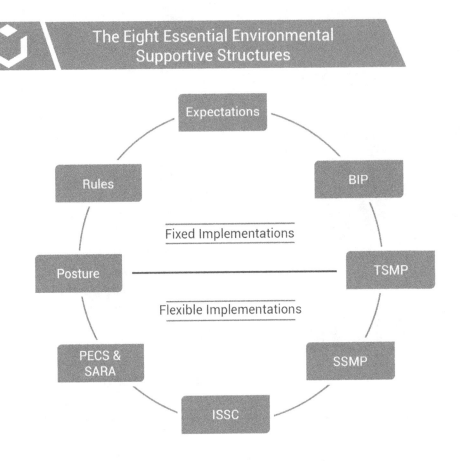

The Eight Essential Environmental Supportive Structures

Expectations

Rules

BIP

Fixed Implementations

Posture

TSMP

Flexible Implementations

PECS & SARA

SSMP

ISSC

There are as many as 25 possible UE101 program implementations. They range from campus and classroom implementations to teacher, staff, and student mediation. These programs are beneficial to the overall long-term achievement of a positive climate of safety and culture of learning and achievement in urban underserved schools. Of these programs, there are eight implementations that are considered non-negotiable. These programs constitute the basic input structure of the UE101 process. The first four are fixed policy and procedures related systems, and the last four are flexible people oriented systems. The non-negotiable programs are as follows:

1. School Posture
2. Rules
3. Expectations
4. Behavior Intervention Plan (BIP)
5. The Teacher-Student Mediation Program
6. The Student-Student Mediation Program
7. The (New) In-School Suspension Classroom Program
8. The Problem, Effect, Cause and Solution (PECS) and the Survey, Analysis, Response and Assessment (SARA) Program

So, let's examine the eight non-negotiable program implementations.

... School posture

====The How!====
SCHOOL POSTURE

FAIRNESS
ACCOUNTABILITY
INTEGRITY
TRUST
HONESTY

We have already had an extensive discussion about school posture and its importance. Therefore, in this section we will simply reiterate a few important points.

As stated, the school posture is the de facto mission. It is the school's guiding light. In the vast "sea of noise," the federal, state and local mandates, your posture should be a beacon of reassurance and stability. It is the one thing all teachers, students, staff, parents, and other community members must be able to count on.

When implemented correctly and reinforced continually, the school posture becomes the school's Constitution, and like the US Constitution, it is ever present and woven into the fabric of everyday life. Just as the Bill of Rights is lodged inside the Constitution, the school's rights and guarantees should be infused into the posture. For example, inside the posture of FAITH, there is a hidden Bill of Rights, so to speak. There is a guarantee of the right to fairness, accountability, integrity, trust, and honesty for all.

Over the years, I have learned that students tend to take these guarantees more seriously than the staff. Staff members in many cases tend to believe that because of their adult status, their position should be the final and uncontested. Although in the overwhelming majority of cases the staff assessment is correct, in California the Education Code guarantees the student an opportunity for review and redress. On countless occasions, therefore, I have had to respectfully listen and respond to students' false claims of impropriety and injustice. The issue, however, was not who was right or wrong, but the fundamental fairness in being heard. When there is an ingrained school posture, I have found that the students appeal less frequently, and the ones who do appeal tend to truly believe their basic guarantees have been violated. For instance, one student felt that he had been so violated he approached me before we could enter my office. "Mr. Lockett," he said, "that teacher broke FAITH with me." Of course, I had to ask, "How?" The response was a dissertation on fairness and trust. According to the student, the teacher did not follow the process as outlined in class. (The outline for the process will be discussed in the section on teacher-student mediation.) The student felt as though the trust between the teacher and himself had been dishonored. It turned out, as it so often does, this was not the case. The true victory was not in the conclusion of the matter but that the process was understood and honored. The student illustrated stage one of restorative justice in schools: gaining a commitment—capturing of hearts and minds. He had process buy-in. Posture is paramount!

... Rules and Expectations and BIP

With the school posture as the guiding light, the next essential steps are to develop a common set of rules, expectations, and a schoolwide behavior intervention plan. It is imperative to develop these entities. Together, they make up the top four (4) fixed non-negotiable UE101 policies and procedures. Rules and expectations can easily be incorporated into one crystal clear document. A straightforward Rule and Expectation graphic follows:

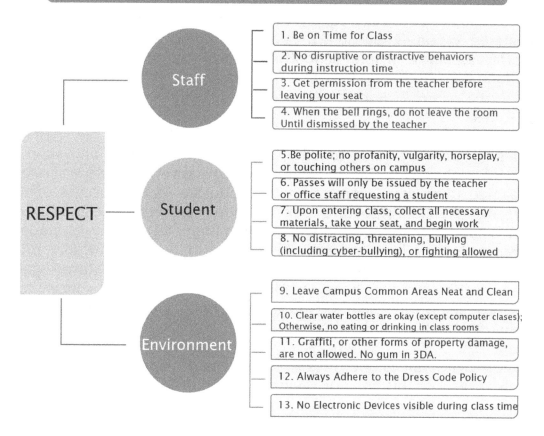

Respect was the only rule for Discovery High School, an alternative school in the Natomas (CA) Unified School District. The school expectations were used to identify the behavioral preferences expected of all students. While the posture stands alone as the de facto mission, rules and expectations are the more specific policies and procedures. They are the entities that activate, animate, and support the posture. They establish a site's norms (the behavior desired and specific guidance pertaining to the desired conduct). The rules and expectations simultaneously serve as a clear and articulated root to the BIP for discipline (discipleship) — which is, and ought to be, to correct, educate, guide, instruct, prepare, and teach, not to punish. Rules and expectations are on the ground, visible, everyday guides to appropriate behavior, conduct, and decorum. At a minimum, every school site must have these elements.

The most important part of the implementation of the policies and procedures is how they are established. How your rules and expectations are created usually determines the level of adherence to and sustainability of them. These policies and procedures work best when they are developed in true collaboration, and when they are implemented, championed, and monitored throughout by thoughtful staff that has embraced the principles of RJ in schools. Rules and expectations specifically satisfy the mandate for Stage 2: Developing a Shared Vision—knowing where we are going and why, and Stage 4: Developing a Whole School Approach—putting it all together, realignment of school policy with new practice.

... **Rules**

Rules perform the same function as laws. They identify and support our lofty objectives. Staying with the legislative example, rules are designed to create an environment conducive to the success of the citizenry. A school's posture is designed to create a climate and culture that is conducive to teaching and learning ultimately leading to student success. Just as laws are created to support our constitution, rules should lead affiliates to echo and support the school posture. Again, they are the norms for behavior. It is crucial the rules be concise and few. Too many rules, like too many laws, create ambiguity, complexity, misunderstanding, and strife.

In most cases, one or two rules are sufficient. Horace Mann would most likely agree with this position. Mann, who is considered the father of the public-school movement, was a Unitarian. That is, he believed that a morally good exploit was one that helped the greatest number of people. Therefore, he believed that all children should theoretically be entitled to an education. As discussed, he established the Common School Movement, which trained teachers to teach students in a uniform fashion and to move the thinking away from education being a domain for just the elite. Common School was said to be established to "mitigate class conflict, circumvent anarchy, enhance civic engagement, and [perhaps most importantly] inculcate moral habits, all by molding society's most malleable members." [36] This does not sound like someone who would be interested in punishment through a plethora of school rules.

Although I found no evidence Mann was absolutely against corporal punishment, he was clearly against one type. Mann vehemently argued and urged that punishment not be used to correct "academic errors." In other words, don't whip the students for misspelling words or getting a math problem wrong. He recommended "encouragement and kindness," dare I say inspiration. I agree with this position, and would go a step further and say that, as educators, we legally stand in loco parentis, which in essence makes us the parent while students are at school. That being the case, the question arises, how do you want your child treated at school? In general, I would not want my son whipped for academic inaccuracy either. In an effort at full disclosure, I must admit that as a parent, I am an advocate of corporal punishment for discipline. When cerebral measures failed, I sparingly used it with my son. Like the boot camp tact officers, I used it as an attention-getting, full-stop, redirection measure designed to correct, mold, and shape my son's character. It was always accompanied by a full discussion of the predicament. My principal belief in corporal punishment derives from biblical teachings. Mine is clearly a minority opinion. It is off the table in public school, and I absolutely accept that position. I do, however, think that many schools are off the chain when it comes to bad behavior because students realize that it's not a consideration. Subsequently, if corporal punishment is not on the menu, there better be effective alternatives available. The UE101 USIP is that alternative.

It is abundantly clear our current system of discipline in schools is modeled after the criminal justice system. The CJ model draws its thrust from penal codes and punitive laws. In California, for example, the rules for schools are codified in the California Education Code. Consequences for infractions are usually limited to warnings, suspensions, and expulsions. Recently, however, Assembly Bill 1729 was passed. The bill was an attempt to restrain the overbearing punitive system by offering additional interventions and strategies for discipline.[37] AB1729 requires that districts and schools install and implement "other means of correction" before proceeding to suspensions and expulsion. By the way, Restorative Justice is now mentioned as one of the alternatives. So how did we get here?

The current student punishment system appears to be a twentieth century invention. It seems to have been a reaction to Dr. Benjamin Spock's 1940's child rearing theory and techniques. Spock, in his book, *Baby and Child Care*, claimed that it was important to make your child feel "special." Prior to then, parents did not bombard children with affection and affirmation. It was commonly believed that an overabundance of affection would "make them weak and unprepared for the world." Children were to be seen and not heard, and corporal punishment was the norm. Spock was also against corporal punishment and advocated demonstrating love and praising children for their uniqueness and exceptionality. In short, he was an advocate of children being seen and thoroughly heard. He also encouraged parents to "follow their instincts, be attentive to the baby's needs, and be generous with affection."[38]

Somewhere around the 1960's, it appears our chickens began to come home to roost, or maybe a better analogy is we began to reap what we had sown. Either way, during the late 1960's or early 1970's, things started changing. Students became more disruptive and violent on campus. Some researchers blamed the transformation, and the subsequent crack down, on a failure in the family dynamic. Television sex and violence and illegal drug use were also identified as potential culprits. Whatever the case, student behavior declined, especially in urban underserved school locations. Many schools became infested with knuckleheads portraying themselves as thugs and gang members. Serious crimes were being committed on school campuses across the country. As a reaction to the crime surge, we responded with zero tolerance policies.[39] AB1729 and another measure, AB420—a bill that I testified against at the Sacramento State Capitol— were countermeasures to zero tolerance. AB 420, at its initial reading, would have eliminated all suspension for students for disruption and defiance. I was definitely not in favor of taking suspension completely off the table. The final bill eliminated suspensions for students in kindergarten through the third grade for disruption and defiance, and it also eliminated expulsions in all grades based solely on disruption.[40] The pendulum has clearly begun to swing again. Therefore, our approach to rules and expectations should reflect the new standard. Rules must be clear, concise, and non-punitive.

... Expectations

According to Webster's dictionary, expectation is defined as a belief that something will happen or is likely to happen; a feeling or belief about how successful, good, etc., someone or something will be.[41] Expectations by their nature are non-punitive. They are, simply put, the epitome and embodiment of the rules. They are our greatest hope for the rules. Again, if rules are the norms, expectations are the school's mores. They are the site's specific ethics, principles, standards, and values. Expectations identify the desired or ideal state of achieving the school posture. Expectations give the rules life and legs.

Think of it this way. Rules and expectations are the new or alternative way of thinking about crime and the avoidance of punishment. Education Code, which is written punitively, clearly identifies the crimes, and then provides guidelines for the consequences. For instance, a student who fights is described as follows:

48900. A pupil shall not be suspended from school or recommended for expulsion, unless the superintendent of the school district or the principal of the school in which the pupil is enrolled determines that the pupil has committed an act as defined pursuant to any of subdivisions (a) to (r), inclusive: (a) (1) Caused, attempted to cause, or threatened to cause physical injury to another person. (2) Willfully used force or violence upon the person of another, except in self-defense.

For the infractions, depending upon the severity, a student may be suspended for up to five days or brought forward for expulsion. This policy was obviously written by lawyers and written to serve the criminal justice model. The only discretion that is left to the individual districts and schools is to determine the number of days up to five and whether to expel.

Let's be clear, I'm not advocating anything as drastic as the elimination of consequences. I am advocating a change in the way we think about our kids and what it means to hold them accountable. There may have been a point in time where a five-day suspension was a valid method of accountability. Today suspension is not necessarily a consequence for many students, thus it is an invalid or illegitimate accountability measure. Different expectation measures must be established and aligned with the school BIP, which will be discussed after this section on expectations.

As with the rules, expectations must be developed in collaboration with, and supported by, all staff and affiliates who are "expected" to be governed by them. One of the major reasons we require so many laws in our society today, and continue to have so many violators, is we don't have proper incentive or proper buy-in to society's expectations. As in RJ Stage 1, we fail to gain commitment and therefore do not capture the hearts and minds of the citizenry. Our general response to a lack of buy-in is to double down. We do this by creating even more laws. This approach is great for entities and individuals like lawyers and gang members, who capitalize on the loopholes, but it wreaks havoc on schools.

There should be more expectations than rules, but not too many of them either. Anything beyond ten expectations is probably overkill. The only way I would ever suggest more is if they were designed to forge consensus and/or to satisfy an urgent legal mandate.

Expectations should parallel the legal system. Why? It is because, at times, it is necessary for a crossover between the two. When access to the legal system, usually via police is required, there should be an accessible, easy, and fluid flow between the two. While nobody desires students to attend schools under a police state model, we do want the ability and capacity for cooperation and a pathway to the legal system when necessary. So, when writing your expectations, make certain they are easily translatable and contain a cooperative pathway to Education Code and, when possible, to the Penal Code.

Here are a few examples taken from Discovery High School, in the Natomas Unified School District, Natomas (CA), where I served as principal. We had 13 expectations. And, boy, did we have a vigorous debate over a number as large as 13, but that's another story. Expectation number 2 was "No disruptive or distractive behavior during instructional time." There are many ways to debate how the expectation could have been drafted—whether more positive and proactive or stringent and legalistic. We could talk all day long about the use of positive and affirmative language, which can be accomplished in the development. At the end of the day, however, we do need the expectations to be easily translatable to Education Code. In this case, expectation 2 is linked to 48900K (disruption/defiance). Likewise, expectation 5, "Be polite, no profanity, vulgarity, horseplay or inappropriate touching on campus" is linked directly to 48900I (profanity/vulgarity). Lastly, expectation 11 informs that "Graffiti or other forms of property damage are not allowed." This expectation is linked to 48900f (damage to school or private property). Our expectation number 1 was a petition to be on time for class. Although it is a good character trait to possess, there is little or no link in this expectation to the legal system. In California Ed Code 48321, there is the School Attendance Review Board (SARB) that attempts to address the matter. Expectation 2 may rise to the level of a penal code violation, and expectations 5 and 11 could make the crossover depending on the nature of the incident.

The illustration that follows is a graphic created by Colonel Mitchell Paige Middle School in La Quinta, California. They linked their posture and rule into one measure. They also made a clear connection between the posture, rules, expectations, education and possibly penal codes. Lastly, the most exquisite and potentially inspirational aspect of the document is the affirming language that was utilized

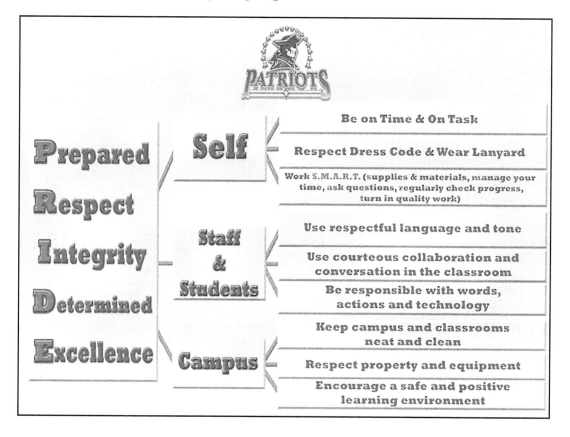

The final graphic, as it relates to expectations and their relationship to the school posture, comes from Sierra Pacific High School, in the Hanford Joint Union High School district. At Sierra Pacific, they took the relational connection even a step further and made it a teaching tool. Not only did they tie in the school posture of ASPIRE with their rule, HONOR, and their expectations, they went a step further and labeled them as such. Then they went on to define the terms and used them as an indoctrinational tool to assist in the RJ in School Communities, Stage 1 process of capturing hearts and minds and promoting buy-in.

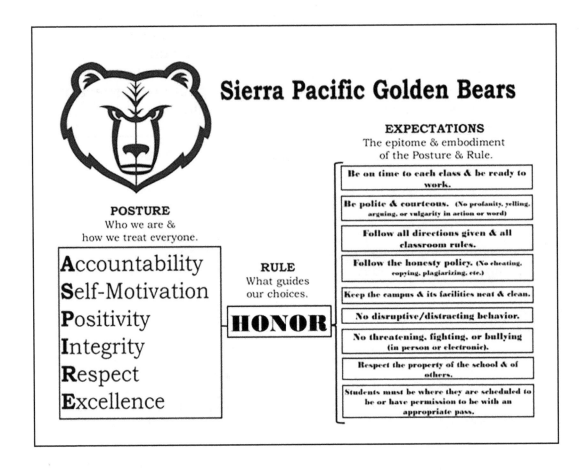

Encapsulating them in context along with your school posture and rules is brilliant and something that I never thought of. Mitchell Paige and Sierra Pacific apparently did, and it produced something quite remarkable. Clear expectations are paramount for two reasons. First, as stated eloquently by Sierra Pacific, they are the epitome and embodiment of the school posture and rules. In other words, they tell you what is needed to satisfy the attitude and outlook of the school posture. Secondly, they make the school's behavior intervention plan more accurate and less ambiguous.

... The Behavior Intervention Plan (BIP)

Most educators are accustomed to a BIP as part of a more intensive intervention and monitoring protocol for special education students. It is a functional, actionable guideline for managing behavior in order to position a special needs student to receive the best educational services possible. A BIP is often part of a student's Individualized Education Plan (IEP), and it could include methods for changing or adapting the climate and culture in hopes of modifying a student's behavior. The special education BIP might employ positive reinforcement to promote good behavior, a planned ignoring strategy to avoid reinforcing bad behavior, and supports needed so the student will not be driven to act out due to frustration or fatigue.[42] So why couldn't we apply this concept to an entire school? Well, I think we can.

At UE101, when we talk BIP, we mean a behavioral intercession system as part of a comprehensive strategy that includes the entire campus as part of a detailed sequential plan of inventions and steps. This is similar or related to Response to Intervention (RTI), which is "a multi-tier approach to the early identification and support of students with learning and behavior needs." The RTI process begins with high-quality instruction and universal screening of all students in the general education classroom. Struggling learners are provided with interventions at increasing levels of intensity to accelerate their rate of learning. These services may be provided by a variety of personnel, including general education teachers, special educators, and specialists. Progress is closely monitored to assess both the learning rate and level of performance of individual students. Educational decisions about the intensity and duration of interventions are based on individual student response to instruction. RTI is designed for use when making decisions in both general education and special education, creating a well-integrated system of instruction and intervention guided by student outcome data.[43]

Our notion of a BIP satisfies or fulfills the RTI for behavioral needs. Instead of employing a punitive disciplinary method designed for crime and punishment, it is designed to recognize the harm done because of the infringement and then work to restore the breach in the relationship. In short, it is designed for discipleship. The BIP does not preclude or replace special education mandates as part of an IEP or any other general education interventional strategies like student study teams, school psychologist evaluations, counselor assessments, or social/case worker involvement. On the contrary, it enhances the other interventions, as it provides normality and standardization. All affiliates—students, teachers, staff, parents and other community partners—become clearer on the student restoration process or campus operational procedures.

When considering the typical discipline plan or discipline matrix, I'm certain this is a different way of thinking about things. In most plans, it plays out something like this. The student gets in trouble; he or she is sent away for punishment; it doesn't change the behavior; the teacher gets pissed; and because the administrators don't have a resolution, the teacher gets blamed for not effectively managing classroom discipline. Trust me, in our system this is not the case. In our system, the BIP is about the restorative nature that exists in all of us. I'm going out on a limb here. I would wager that 99.999 percent of all school affiliates desire that every student succeeds. I won't even bother to address the .001 percent. If I am correct, why do we use such punitive measures in hopes of changing student behavior? Is it because it works so well in our penal—police, probation, prison and parole—system? My sarcastic ire rises. But seriously, how can our students succeed if they feel like outcasts and we treat them like criminals?

As community members and parents, restoration is already scorched into our DNA. We must be the initiators of it in our schools. The answer is clearly not to use a bigger, harder hammer to beat students into submission. We should, we must, strive to teach our students to be pursuers of reconciliation and restoration as part of their character and integrity. Therefore, in underserved schools, we must be inspirational instructional leaders. And the beautiful part about the entire thing is that we already know how to do it. We do it at home with our families all the time. We must also do it in our educational institutions.

One of the greatest compliments I received about our process came from a school counselor in Merced, California. A short time after participating in one of our workshops, he sent me an email describing how he had created a posture, rules, expectations and a BIP for his family. (Although I am certain that, as with most families, there were already a set of unspoken beliefs, expectations and values. In his case, he had taken the time to codify them.) The counselor went on to say that his course of action was working beautifully. I'm not surprised by the outcome. For most people, it is a natural thing to be restorative rather than punitive and retributive with your family. Just think about it, how often do you suspend or ban your child from home for five days? As much as some of you may want to do it, the answer of course is never. In fact, for many of you a one hour timeout is considered cruel and unusual punishment. So, why then are we so open to the notion of more severe actions against other people's children? It may be because of the relationship breach. It is easier to banish someone who is not seen as a member of your collective from the start. All I propose here is that similar restorative courtesy be extended to urban underserved students.

So, this is what a BIP might look like at your school. While many plans typically use a two-step model involving the teacher and the administrators, at UE101 we recommend three steps—the teacher/staff, the ISSC, and the administrator. But we shouldn't get hung up on the steps because, like in dancing, it's not about how many steps or moves you got, it's more about how they're choreographed that makes the dance flow. So, allow me to describe or choreograph the process. Although behavioral issues are usually thought of in terms of the teacher and student, an incident could originate with any staff member. The important point here is to understand the process should be the same. That's correct—with our process, any staff member can initiate the procedure, and all should be prepared to engage students whenever a breach or infringement occurs. For the sake of illustrative simplicity, I will presuppose the issue began in the classroom and was initiated by a student's disruptive conduct.

In our process, the teacher is required to execute three interventional steps: issue a warning, offer an invitation to correct through the mediation process, and direct the student to leave the classroom. Here is how the process should advance. Whenever a teacher believes it is necessary to start the process, a warning is conveyed. The most important aspect of the warning is not that it is issued, but how it is issued. It should be issued with the intention of building a better relationship. Therefore, a warning should be framed in positive terms. Consequently, it should be issued as an invitation and opportunity to self-correct behavior and to resume normal interactions as part of the group. The warning should, for that reason, be polite and professional. It should be issued without a browbeating and should only take a few seconds to deliver.

After the warning is given, in order to demonstrate the academic urgency, the teacher should immediately return to the lesson or whatever activity the class is engaged in. If the student self-corrects, the only other thing that might occur is a friendly posture-reinforcing reminder towards the end of class. For example: the teacher might say, everyone knows we take our posture of FAITH seriously around here, and we expect fairness to be extended to all. As the student leaves class, the teacher might shake his or her hand and articulate that he is looking forward to working together the next time they are in class.

If the behavior does not improve after the warning, the next intervention should be an offer to correct the behavior through the mediation process. When the warning fails, the teacher provides the student with a Teacher-Student Mediation Program (TSMP) form. We recommend that the form be printed in a distinctive color for easy recognition. (The TSMP process will be discussed in greater detail later.)

Whenever the form is issued, it triggers an automatic invitation to an after-school mediation conference with the teacher. (Because the program features are to be meticulously front end loaded, all students should be fully aware and understand the process prior to receiving the form. Therefore, there should be no need for an extended discussion at the time of issuance.) The student should accept the form, complete it, and modify their behavior.

If the student refuses the form or continues the infringement, step three of the process is initiated. At this point, the student is asked to take the colorful TSMP form and proceed to the In-School Suspension Classroom (ISSC). (The ISSC process will be discussed in greater detail later.) As the student is leaving the classroom, the teacher should attempt to make it an inspirational moment. This may be achieved by encouraging the student to resolve their concern as quickly as possible in order to be reunited with the class. The teacher should also offer a positive reminder of the after-school mediation meeting. The entire interaction time for a behavioral matter with a student during class instruction time should last no more than one minute; two minutes is too long.

So, what are the benefits of this process? There are many. The main benefits are that the process is inspirational and instructional. It also goes a long way towards the fulfillment of the five stages of restorative justice in school. Not only is the process inspirational and instructional, it is never punitive. Also, the expressed and intended goals for the intervention, to safeguard and protect the instructional environment and the building of relationships, are achieved. As far as the fulfillment of the stages of RJ in schools, the process clearly satisfies stages 3, 4 and 5—the Development of Responsive and Effective Practice, a Whole School Approach and Developing Professional Relationships. Finally, the process reinforces the school posture.

At every stage in the process, the teacher also has an opportunity to inspire and encourage the student to embrace the procedure for building a better relationship. Further, the teachers gain a greater sense of confidence, as they recognize there is a process, and it supports their intended goal of providing quality instruction in an environment conducive to teaching and learning. I am convinced the achievement gap is not due to a lack of teacher training. Instead, I believe it is the byproduct of a loss of instructional minutes due to class disruptions. From my experience and observations, it only takes a few well-placed knuckleheads devouring about ten instructional minutes per period to destroy the school's culture of learning and achievement. With this process, the learning is not as impeded because it does not stop during a corrective intervention. Then, when the student returns for the mediation meeting after school, it provides the perfect atmosphere and opportunity for the teacher to forge a positive new relationship that can carry over to classroom. Another positive attribute of the program is that the meeting takes place off stage; that is, without a classroom audience. Therefore, there is no competition for student loyalty, less regrouping, and fewer instructional minutes lost.

As the student proceeds to the ISSC, there is one additional benefit that occurs. Because of the provocative color of the form, which doubles as a hall pass, everyone is made aware of why the student is out of class and where the student should be going. Furthermore, because of the student's conspicuousness, any staff member—from the campus supervision (security) to custodians, administrators, clerical, counselors and prep-time teachers—who encounters the student has a built-in set up to encourage the student and reinforce the importance of adherence to the process. And, if that person so chooses, while inspiring and encouraging, they could also provide an escort to the ISSC. This would reduce excessive aimless student wandering on campus.

In brief, the TSMP serves as an in-class intervention strategy, an after-school procedure for mediation and relationship building, and an on-campus staff notification tool. To go one step further, if it is coupled with a clear and distinctive restroom pass strategy, aimless wandering and excessive foot traffic would, for all practical purposes, be eliminated. I always stress, and factually assert, that when using this system, it cuts the foot traffic down to two types—one consists of the students headed for the ISSC and the other for the restroom. I jokingly refer to everyone else as a potential terrorist until proven otherwise. But seriously, the TSMP changes the climate as it applies to safety and boosts the potential for a successful culture through positive relationship building.

Once in the ISSC, the school BIP identifies the prescribed protocol the staff and student should follow. It normally entails a combination of the following strategies: a sign-in procedure, the completion and/or submitting of the TSMP form, an assignment of classwork (preferably based upon test prep materials), an individual and/or group counseling session, and an after-school intervention protocol. We also recommend a positive conditional counseling follow-up session. This can easily be facilitated through the creation of an ISSC counseling caseload. Lastly, a reminder of the student's obligation to return to the original teacher for a mediation meeting should be given.

The BIP should also include a section for administrative interventions. If a student arrives at the office of the assistant/vice principal or the principal, there should be an understanding that one of two scenarios has occurred—there was either a very serious incident (drugs, explosives, fight, sexual battery, weapons, etc.) and the ISSC was bypassed or the student has run the intervention table (teacher and ISSC interventions). Under these circumstances, it should make the administrator's choices and options relatively straightforward. It should also make their traditional workload much lighter. Strategies that might be accessible to administrators include, but are not limited to, a student conference, a parent conference, a return to the ISSC, supervised campus beautification, counseling, home suspension, a combination of strategies (some home and some ISSC suspension), or the expulsion process. Of course, a school may want to add more or fewer interventions; the final number of interventions is determined by each individual school. The inset that follows illustrates a potential outline of interventions that might be incorporated into a BIP:

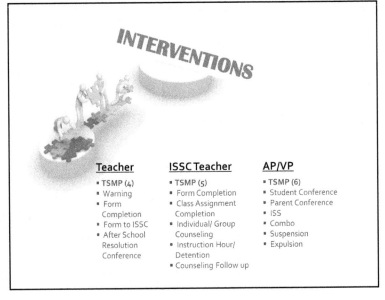

Teacher	ISSC Teacher	AP/VP
• TSMP (4)	• TSMP (5)	• TSMP (6)
• Warning	• Form Completion	• Student Conference
• Form Completion	• Class Assignment Completion	• Parent Conference
• Form to ISSC	• Individual/ Group Counseling	• ISS
• After School Resolution Conference	• Instruction Hour/ Detention	• Combo
	• Counseling Follow up	• Suspension
		• Expulsion

Although the interventional outline of the BIP—the teacher, ISSC, and the administrator measures —and the slate of interventions are crucial to the program's success, another feature, the supportive structure, is perhaps of more importance. While the interventional outline of the program addresses who is responsible for the interventions, the interventional structure deals with when and how the strategies and interventions will occur. If we went all the way back to the Relationship and Resource analogy discussed earlier, it would be easy to see this entire process is all about the relationship aspect of the model. Relationships, as you will recall, are divided into two parts: leadership and structure. The people and interventional parts of the BIP fit perfectly into the inspirational and instructional realm. When we get to the section on how the interventions are meted out, you will see that it draws its impetus from the structural component of relationships. This includes mostly the physical layout, but it leaves room for fraternal structures.

The physical structure of the BIP is of tremendous importance, as it is the glue that holds together the who and what of the process. All the disagreements and disputes I can recall between teachers and administrators usually came down to who and what. Who was supposed to do something and what it was believed they were supposed to be doing. Sometimes it goes like this: the administrator tells the teacher, you were supposed to do this, that, and the other . . . and the teacher responds, well you were supposed to do this, this, this and this. And you know what—they are usually both correct. The impediment in these situations is usually that neither has a clear structure on how or when they are supposed to do it. This system removes the ambiguity. We addressed that issue by creating a simple how to structure. The graphic that follows illustrates the who, what, and the structural how. It is presented in the form of a process flow chart.

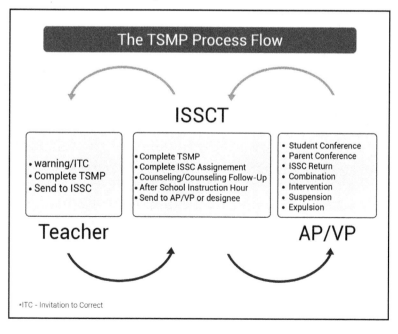

From the chart, it is easy to see that the teacher (who) provides the interventions (what) and the order (when). If the interventions are ineffective, the arrow clearly directs the student to the next layer of interventions. The student leaves the classroom and goes to the ISSC. If the student's performance does not improve, and he or she does not correct and redirect while in the ISSC as indicated by the second arrow, they proceed to an administrator.

Here is where our process makes a dramatic departure from the norm. Whether a student goes home on suspension, has a change of heart and agrees to embrace the process, is sent to debrief with a counselor, or begins something drastic like the expulsion process, it does not matter. Upon completion of the interventional steps, it is necessary for the student to go through the system in reverse. In other words, after a home suspension, instead of going directly back to class, the student must go back to the ISSC. The reason for the reverse return process should be clear. It's a proving ground, and it's also an opportunity to make things right throughout the system. A significant problem I have observed often occurs in the aftermath of a suspension. In many cases, and especially with urban underserved students, suspension is not a negative consequence or intervention. Therefore, after the suspension, when students return to class, they walk back into the room triumphantly. This creates the misconception that the student is bulletproof. The return process frequently undermines the teacher's authority. With our system, the teacher is the final voice in a return to his or her classroom.

Our process provides that if a student is sent from class to the ISSC, and then from the ISSC to an administrator, and then sent home on suspension, the return process must be reversed. The student, with or without a parent conference (as determined by the administrator), shall return to the administrator's office. After a debriefing, the administrator sends the student to the ISSC. The check-in with the ISSC can verify that the TSMP and other interventions were completed. Also, to be sent from the ISSC to the administrator usually means that the relationship breach which occurred in the ISSC needs to be resolved. When the ISSC teacher clears the student, it is then necessary for the student to meet with the original teacher at the end of the day for their mediation prior to returning to class. (This may not require that the student remain in the ISSC for the entire day, but it assures the student will not return to the original teacher's classroom triumphantly.) The procedure ultimately protects the climate of safety while forging better relationships and placing special emphasis on the importance of a culture of learning.

Now let's take a quick look at the fraternal processing. The physical or structural processing is a roadmap of what will occur in the disciplining (discipleship) of a student. The fraternal processing deals with the attitude taken when disciplining— it's the how. This is a great place to revisit and discuss what is meant by discipline.

When we use the term discipline, it is vitally important for us to determine what we really mean. I am certain when the original framers of the public education movement, such as Horace Mann, Henry Adams and John Dewey, used the term discipline, they had discipleship in mind. In fact, when John Dewey spoke of discipline, he spoke of it in this manner: Formal discipline refers both to the outcome of trained power and to the method of training through repeated exercise. The forms of power in question are such things as the faculties of perceiving, retaining, recalling, associating, attending, willing, feeling, imagining, thinking, etc., which are then shaped by exercise upon material presented.[44] They clearly meant the discipleship of students, not punishment.

A disciplined individual as defined by the Merriam-Webster dictionary is one who accepts and assists in spreading the doctrines of another . . . [A] convinced adherent of a school or individual.[45] While they clearly meant discipleship, we have bastardized the word discipline to the point where it is defined as punishment. To change the outcome for urban underserved students, we rekindle our belief about the true meaning and nature of discipline. We must begin to view discipline as "training that corrects, molds, or perfects the mental faculties or moral character."[46]

If you recall, while outlining the role of the teacher in this progression, I mentioned a bit about attitude towards the student. Here is the language that I used: *As the student is leaving the classroom, the teacher should attempt to make it an inspirational moment. This may be achieved by encouraging the student to resolve their concern as quickly as possible in order to be reunited with the class.* This verbiage is all about fraternization. And I must say, I don't see enough of it. In fact, it never ceases to amaze me the number of staff members who still attempt to discipline through intimidation and threats of punishment, even when it is ineffective. It's kind of like talking louder to a deaf person, then punishing them for not hearing you. We know the answer is not to talk louder; the answer is to learn to sign. That would be a second order change. This is what we are proposing. Fraternizing through authentic relationships with urban underserved students is a course change. And the change must start with you, not the student.

UE101

At UE101, we always recommend and dedicate a portion of our workshops to the changing of the staff's communication style. We call it "Let's Talk Language." In this session, the participants work on skills like ridding themselves of unsupportive language such as sarcasm and negative comparisons and replacing it with positive affirmations, greater specificity, concrete language, and appropriate level vocabulary. There is also a session on non-verbal communication and the importance of facial expressions, tone, and body language. I said all of that to say this: society has made a clear and dramatic shift. To successfully engage and educate our urban underserved emergent student population, academia must also make a change. In short, it's time for the old dogs to learn a few new tricks.

How you communicate with kids, whether yours or someone else's, matters. How you interact with students is at the heart of fraternization. It's the interpersonal structural communication piece that leads to the instructional piece. Simply put, people function better and are more productive in restorative climates and cultures. Do not be misled—changing the way one fraternizes is not easy. In fact, I think it can be as tough as learning Arabic or Chinese because it involves the abandoning of deep seated feelings and emotions. But the beautiful thing about learning to fraternize is that it is fully attainable by everyone. And the benefits are enormous.

Fraternization is essential for the development of authentic relationships. At every stage of the educational process, students must interact with adults. It is my greatest hope that each adult staff member they encounter is an inspirational instructional leader. For them to be inspirational, they must be authentic. Genuine fraternization is authenticity on display. Now back to the BIP.

When your school's BIP comes together, it may take many forms. The only suggestion I offer is this: simplicity. The simpler it is the better. Beyond keeping it simple, make sure all aspects or staff affiliates—administrative, certificated and classified—are included in its development process. In addition, you should make certain all students and staff fully understand the procedure. This understanding can be easily accomplished through student-led daily public intercom announcements, assemblies, posters, classroom warmups and on-campus staff to student fraternization. A few examples of school BIPs are included.

Behavior Intervention Plan (BIP)
Responsibility and Interventions:

Teachers / Staff	In-School Suspension Classroom Teacher (ISSCT) / Chief of Student Affairs (COSA)	KLA Plus (ISSC Program)
Violation 1: ▪Verbal Warning	**Visitation 1:** ▪Incident documentation ▪TSMP form completed. (Student remains in the ISSC for remainder of block. If student refuses to complete form, a parent conference is scheduled. Student is sent home or remains in the ISSC for remainder of the school day.)	Student may be assigned to the In-school Suspension Classroom (ISSC) in accordance with CA Ed. Code (Sect.48911.1)
Violation 2: ▪Verbal Warning ▪ Student completes Teacher-Student Mediation Program (TSMP) form	**Visitation 2:** ▪Incident documentation ▪TSMP form completed. ▪One (1) hour (after school) Detention ▪Parent Call (Student remains in the ISSC for remainder of block. If student refuses to complete form, a parent conference must be scheduled. The student will be sent home, or remains in the ISSC for remainder of the school day.)	▪ A student may be assigned ISSC for up to 5 days ▪Core Course Program (MSHE)- all subject coursework will be completed ▪Counseling (Mandatory) (Additional counseling services may be determined and issued by the KLA Counseling Office.) ▪Lunch will be taken in the ISSC
Violation 3: ▪Refusal to complete TSMP, student is sent to the In-School Suspension Classroom (ISSC)	**Visitation 3:** ▪Incident documentation ▪TSMP form completed. ▪One (1) hour Detention, In-school Suspension, Suspension ▪Parent Call, and Conference (Student may be assigned to ISSC. Student is sent home or remains in the ISSC for remainder of the school day.)	**Suspension / Removal Process** ▪The KLA Suspension/ Expulsion Policy will be exercised.
Note: At the teacher's _**discretion**_, a student may be sent to the ISSC for any violation of the School Rules and Expectation Policy.	**Note:** For more serious violations, the COSA may send a student home pending a parent conference, ISSC, Saturday school, suspension, or expulsion.	

A.S.P.I.R.E.

SPHS Behavioral Intervention Plan BIP
Responsibilities and Interventions

STAFF RESPONSIBILITIES: Correcting Student Behavior	
Step 1 Staff gives verbal warning. **NOTE:** This must occur EACH time a behavior needs correction.	**Step 2** Staff gives student the SP Teacher-Student ITT form. Student choosing to fill out the ITT form correctly will stay in class and mediate with the staff member as soon as possible. Teacher decides time of meeting on ITT form. Student choosing to Not Work the Program (NWP) will be sent to the IC Room. NWP includes: • Refusing to fill out ITT form. • Failure to complete ITT form. • Using inappropriate, disrespectful, or profane language on the ITT form. • Being disrespectful or disruptive while completing the ITT form. • Refusing to mediate with the staff member.

STUDENT IS REQUIRED TO BRING THE ITT FORM TO THE Intervention Center. If student does not bring the ITT form to the Intervention Center and/or renders the form unusable, student will spend the remainder of the day in the Intervention Center.

NOTE: A student will be sent immediately to administration for any serious violation including, but not limited to fighting, drugs, alcohol, vandalism, and/or severe disrespect to a staff member. ***For more serious violations, administration may send a student home pending a parent conference, IC Room or suspension.

Any students involved in co-curricular or extracurricular activities are NOT eligible to participate that day if sent to the IC Room.

INTERVENTIONS (Per Semester): IC Room		
1st Violation • Incident documented. • ITT form completed. Student remains in the IC Room for remainder of period. If student refuses to complete ITT form or is sent to the office for choosing to not meet IC Room expectations: • Student is sent home OR remains in the Intervention Center for the remainder of the day. • Student serves an additional 7 periods (1 school day) in the Intervention Center.	**2nd Violation** • Incident documented. • ITT form completed. • Parent contacted. (IC teacher or Admin) • Student remains in the IC Room for remainder of period AND an additional 3 periods. If student refuses to complete ITT form or is sent to the office for choosing to not meet IC Room expectations: • Parent contact is made by Intervention Center teacher. • Student is sent home OR remains in the Intervention Center for the remainder of the day. • Student serves an additional 7 periods (1 school day) in the Intervention Center.	**3 or more Violations** • Incident documented. • ITT form completed. • Parent contacted by Administration. • Student remains in the IC Room for remainder of period AND an additional 7 periods. If student refuses to complete ITT form or is sent to the office for choosing to not meet IC Room expectations: • Parent contact is made by the administrator. • SST may be scheduled. • Student is sent home OR remains in the Intervention Center for the remainder of the day. • Student serves an additional 7 periods (1 school day) in the Intervention Center.

If a student is sent to IC Room more than one time during the school day, the student will remain there for the remainder of the day.

Should FUTURE EXPECTATIONS be broken for the same violation, an automatic TSMP with administration will take place.

Should more discussion be required, an administrator will automatically be included. A meeting with the teacher will be held prior to the TSMP taking place. If necessary, the Restorative Circle will grow until resolved.

INTERVENTIONS: IC Room Program Overview
Student may be assigned In-School Suspension in accordance with CA Ed. Code (Sect.48911.1). • A student may be assigned to IC Room for up to five days. • The IC Room's focus is to help improve academic and social skills. • Counseling is provided: Administrator interaction and counseling is available. • Classwork and homework will be completed. (If none, ICT will provide work)

This BIP is from Sierra Pacific High School (SPHS) in the Hanford Joint Union High School District, Hanford, California. At SPHS, the ISSC is referred to as the IC or Intervention Center; the TSMP is called an ITT or Invitation to Talk form. The term ITT form was created and used by Kingswood K-8 in the San Juan Unified School District, Carmichael, California.

Behavior Intervention Plan BIP
Responsibilities and Interventions

STAFF RESPONSIBILITES: Correcting Student Behavior

Step 1	Step 2
Staff gives verbal warning.	Staff gives student the Valley Staff-Student Mediation Program (VSSMP) form. Student choosing to fill out the VSSMP form correctly will stay in class and mediate with the staff member as soon as possible. Student choosing to **Not Work the Program (NWP)** will be sent to In-School Suspension Classroom (ISSC). **NWP includes:** • Refusing to fill out VSSMP form. • Failure to complete VSSMP form. • Using inappropriate, disrespectful, or profane language on the form. • Being disrespectful or disruptive while completing the VSSMP form. • Refusing to mediate with the staff member. STUDENT IS REQUIRED TO BRING THE VSSMP TO THE ISSC. If student does not bring the VSSMP form to ISSC and/or renders the form unusable, student will spend the remainder of the day in ISSC.

NOTE: A student will be sent immediately to administration for any serious violation including, but not limited to fighting, confrontational behavior, drugs, alcohol, vandalism, severe disrespect to a staff member and/or habitual behavior incidents.

INTERVENTIONS (Per Quarter): In-School Suspension Classroom (ISSC)

1st Violation	2nd Violation	3 or more Violations
• Incident documented. • VSSMP form completed. Student remains in the ISSC for remainder of period.	• Incident documented. • VSSMP form completed. • Parent contacted. • Student remains in the ISSC for remainder of period and an additional 3 periods.	• Incident documented. • VSSMP form completed. • Parent contacted. • Student remains in the ISSC for remainder of period and an additional 7 periods.
If student refuses to complete VSSMP form or is sent to the office for choosing to not meet ISSC expectations: • Student is sent home OR remains in the ISSC for the remainder of the day and serves an additional 7 periods (1 school day) in the ISSC.	If student refuses to complete VSSMP form or is sent to the office for choosing to not meet ISSC expectations: • Parent contact is made by ISSC teacher. • Student is sent home OR remains in the ISSC for the remainder of the day and serves an additional 7 periods (1 school day) in the ISSC.	If student refuses to complete VSSMP form or is sent to the office for choosing to not meet ISSC expectations: • Parent contact is made by the administrator. • Student is sent home OR remains in the ISSC for the remainder of the day and serves an additional 7 periods (1 school day) in the ISSC.

NOTE: For more serious violations, administration may send a student home pending a parent conference, ISSC or suspension.
If a student is sent to ISSC more than one time during the school day, the student will stay in ISSC the remainder of the day.

INTERVENTIONS: ISSC Program Overview

Student may be assigned In-School Suspension in accordance with CA Ed. Code (Sect.48911.1).
• A student may be assigned to ISSC for up to five days.
• ISSC curriculum is to help improve student academic and social skills.
• Counseling provided.

This BIP is from Valley Community Schools in Merced County Office of Education, Merced California. At VCS, the TSMP is referred to as a VSSMP or Valley Staff Student Mediation Program. The VCS BIP also includes a program overview section that makes a direct connection of their ISSC to California Education Code.

Behavior Intervention Plan (BIP)
Responsibility and Interventions

Teachers / Staff	In-School Suspension Classroom (ISSC)/Administrative Designee	CMP Plus (ISSC Program)
Breach1: ▪Verbal Warning	**Visitation 1:** ▪Incident documentation ▪TSMP form completed. (Student remains in the ISSC for remainder of the period. If student refuses to complete form, a parent conference shall be scheduled. Student is sent home or remains in the ISSC for remainder of the school day.)	A Student may be assigned to the In-school Suspension Classroom (ISSC) in accordance with CA Ed. Code (Sect.48911.1)
Breach 2: ▪Verbal Warning ▪ Student completes Teacher-Student Mediation Program (TSMP) form *Student remains in Class, and must meet with the teacher at the end of the school day.*	**Visitation 2:** ▪Incident documentation ▪TSMP form completed. ▪One (1) hour (after school) Tutorial ▪Parent Call (Student remains in the ISSC for remainder of the period. If the student refuses to complete the form, a parent conference must be scheduled. The student will be sent home, or remains in the ISSC for remainder of the school day.)	▪ A student may be assigned ISSC for up to 5 days ▪Core Course Program (Math and English coursework will be completed) ▪Counseling Block (Mandatory) ▪Additional counseling services may be determined and issued by the CMP Counseling Office. ▪Lunch will be taken in the ISSC ▪All students in ISSC at the end of the day must attend tutorial.
Breach 3: ▪Refusal to complete TSMP *Student is sent to the In-School Suspension Classroom (ISSC)*	**Visitation 3:** ▪Incident documentation ▪TSMP form completed. ▪One (1) hour Tutorial, In-school Suspension, Suspension ▪Parent Call, and Conference (Student may be assigned to ISSC. Student is sent home or remains in the ISSC for remainder of the school day.)	
Note: For **serious incidents**, or at the teacher's *discretion*, a student may be sent to the ISSC for any violation of the school's Rules and Expectation Policy.	**Note:** For more serious incidents, the student may be home pending a parent conference, ISSC, Saturday school, suspension, or expulsion.	**Suspension/ Removal Process** ▪The CMP Suspension/ Expulsion Policy shall be exercised as needed.

This BIP is from Colonel Mitchell Paige Middle School, in the Desert Sands Unified School District, La Quinta, California. Paige's BIP contains much of the same content as the others, with a few subtleties. The mere thought of referring to the document as Responsibility and Interventions is one example.

Yosemite Intervention Plan

Staff Daily Responsibilities: Correcting Student Behavior

Step 1	Step 2	Step 3
• Verbal Warning	• Verbal Warning • Student completes "Incident Form" (IF) • Student remains in class • Teacher conferences with student at a later time.	• Student given new IF and sent to IC for the remainder of the day unless otherwise noted by the teacher.

NOTE:
- Staff may begin Incident Form for any violations of any school rules/procedures.
- Students should be sent immediately to an AP for any serious violations including, but not limited to, fighting, confrontational behavior, drugs, alcohol, vandalism, and severe disrespect towards a staff member.

Students choosing to Not Work the Program (NWP) will be sent to IC. The Incident Form must be carried and visible.
NWP includes:
- Refusing or failing to fill out the Incident Form in a timely manner.
- Using inappropriate or disrespectful language on the form.
- Refusing to mediate with the staff member.

Interventions: Intervention Center

1st Violation	2nd Violation	3rd Violation
• Incident documented in ABI. • Incident Form completed. Student remains in IC for remainder of period • Parent contact by IC teacher If student refuses to complete Incident Form, the student is sent to an administrator and parent contact is made. Student is sent home and will serve a day in IC once he/she returns from home suspension.	• Incident documented in ABI • Incident Form completed • Parent contacted by IC teacher • Student remains in the IC for remainder of period and an additional 3 periods If student refuses to complete Incident Form, the student is sent to an administrator and parent contact is made. Student is sent home and will serve a day in IC once he/she returns from home suspension.	• Incident documented in ABI • Incident Form completed • Parent contacted by IC teacher • Student remains in the IC for the remainder of the period and an additional 7 periods If student refuses to complete Incident Form, the student is sent to an administrator and parent contact is made. Student is sent home and will serve a day in IC once he/she returns from home suspension.

4th Violation	5th Violation	6th Violation
• Incident documented in ABI • Incident Form completed • Parent contacted by IC teacher • Student remains in the IC for the remainder of the period and an additional 7 periods If student refuses to complete Incident Form, the student is sent to an administrator and parent contact is made. Student is sent home and will serve a day in IC once he/she returns from home suspension. • Loss of eligibility for extracurricular activities (6 weeks) • Parent Conference and behavior contract	• Incident documented in ABI • Incident Form completed • Parent contacted by IC teacher • Student remains in the IC for the remainder of the period and an additional 7 periods If student refuses to complete Incident Form, the student is sent to an administrator and parent contact is made. Student is sent home and will serve a day in IC once he/she returns from home suspension. • 2 days home suspension and 1 day in IC • Possible referral to ACEs • Possible referral to counseling services • Possible referral to School Psychologist • Remind student of behavioral contract	• Incident documented in ABI • Incident Form completed • Parent contacted by IC teacher • Student remains in the IC for the remainder of the period and an additional 7 periods If student refuses to complete Incident Form, the student is sent to an administrator and parent contact is made. Student is sent home and will serve a day in IC once he/she returns from home suspension. • 3 days home suspension and 1 day in IC • Student Study Team (SST)

DYNAMITE DRAGONS D.R.E.A.M.
DEDICATED RESPECTFUL ENGAGED ACCOUNTABLE MOTIVATED

This last BIP is from Yosemite High School, a continuation school in the Merced Union High School District, Merced California. Besides the noticeable increase in the number of potentional violations, a clear accommodation for the nature of the school, the YHS BIP goes a bit further than the others. It incorporates many of the possible interventional referral services available, primarily listed under the fourth and fifth violations.

From the BIPs observed here, it should be easy to see why the document is necessary. The BIP establishes and sets clear interventional procedures. The procedures lead to better relationships, which leads to greater buy-in, which ultimately leads to stable climate and higher staff and student performance.

Posture, rules, expectations, and BIP are four programs that are vital to the success of any urban underserved school. Now let's take a closer look at the other four essential site program implementations —teacher-student mediation, student-student mediation, the in-school suspension classroom, and PECS and SARA.

... Teacher-Student Mediation Program (TSMP)

The TSMP is the primary process for repairing campus infringements, building relationships, and reconciliation and restoration between teachers and students. This amazing process was developed more than a decade ago while I was working as Dean of students at Gompers Secondary School in San Diego. At that time, I was fortunate to work with a principal who was courageous enough to acknowledge that the status quo was unacceptable. The summer after accepting the position, Principal Mitchell sat me down to discuss the path forward. He told me he was open to trying new and innovative approaches to decreasing campus conflict and violence and improving student achievement. Instead of providing me with an elaborate and vague job description, he sent me away to come up with a model to accomplish that goal. When I returned, he respectfully listened to my thoughts on the potential benefits of incorporating a school climate program based upon the principles of restorative justice. After the discussion, he cleared the way for implementation.

Fortunately for me, I didn't have to create a program from scratch. There was a proliferation of well researched and tested community-based restoration models available. As discussed, I fully understood the concept of Restorative Justice, and the Victim Offender Reconciliation Program (VORP) model. In addition, I was already certified as a mediator and had previously worked as a mediation program manager and trainer. With the VORP experience and training behind me, it made sense for me to design the Gompers program after their model. Further, as a former police officer, if I understood nothing else, I knew forms. In policing, there was a form for everything. My task was to combine the two entities into one cohesive process that was inviting and user friendly.

The initial process was designed for mediation between students only— Student-Student Mediation Program (SSMP). I functioned as the mediator. So, when a dispute arose between students, whether suspended or not, before returning to class, they were sent to me for a mediated resolution and documented agreement.

In the first year of the program, I completed roughly 90 mediations involving approximately 200 students. At the end of the school year, it was clear the program had a profoundly positive impact on our school climate. Campus tension was substantially reduced and there appeared to be no perceptible downside. In fact, from among all the student participants, none ended up in a new physical altercation, and only two of the students returned for follow-up assistance. The follow-up mainly consisted of clarifying their mediated positions. The girls had a hair pulling fight. One of the girls had a hair weave and it had been damaged in the altercation. The other girl, who accepted responsibility for her part in the conflict, agreed to pay half the cost of the repair. The issue was the cost; it was far more than had been estimated. We ended up bringing in the parents—expanding the "restorative circle." After discussion, they came to a new understanding. The agreement was promptly fulfilled. And even more remarkable, the parents found they had common community friends and became friends themselves. Ron Claassen would say, "Blessed are the peacemakers."

In year two of the program, the number of mediations and campus violence incidents dropped exponentially. The number of on-campus fights fell to an unheard-of number—five. That's right! There were only five fights all year. Suspensions dropped by about seventy-five percent. In fact, the suspension rate

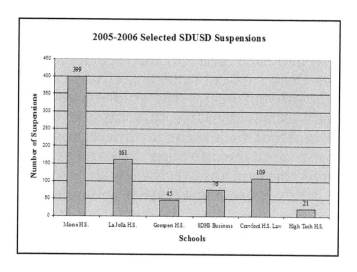

dropped below the State average. For an urban underserved school with a population of approximately 1700 students that was known throughout the district for brawls, rebellions and riots, this was some feat. The graphic that follows is a comparative snapshot of suspension data for 2005. Morse's data reflected the entire comprehensive population. SDHS and Crawford had divided into a small model. Their data represents one school within a site that might contain as many as four small schools. La Jolla High School is the flagship of the SDUSD. And High Tech High was an arm-of-the-district charter; for the most part, it had the advantage of selectivity.

Observing the potential benefits of the program, Mr. Mitchell asked if I would attempt to come up with a process that could be used directly in the classroom between teachers and students. I instantly knew that would pose something of a challenge.

He was asking me to train all the teachers to be mediators of their own conflicts, then to lead their potential offenders through a reconciliation process culminating in a documented resolution agreement. Although I had never heard of it being done before, I thought it was a brilliant idea and an exciting opportunity.

I didn't encounter much resistance from the students. The teachers were a different story. Many of the students already understood the process and had been a part of the mediations conducted the previous year in the Dean's office. Until this effort, I had failed to make an important student-staff nexus. The students who had problems with each other were usually the same students who had problems with their teachers. Because of their frequent interactions with the system, they usually understood the discipline cycle and sequence better than the teachers. I think this explains why the students appeared to take the consequences in stride, while many teachers often felt dissatisfied with the outcomes. For the most part, teachers simply wanted to teach without being burdened by what they saw as unnecessary student disruptions and pointless administrative initiatives and add-ons. When considering the track record of failed improvement strategies, the attitudes were somewhat justified. Therefore, with many of them predisposed to view any new process as just another unnecessary, cumbersome administrative mandate, I knew it had to be relatively easy to incorporate and, above all, it had to be effective if the teachers were to embrace and implement the program.

Every step of the way, right down to the name of the program—teacher-student mediation—I was very careful not to offend or alienate teachers. By putting the teacher first (and they are and ought to be), it gave them assurance the program was not just another train-and-blame tactic. Instead it was about casting teachers in the role of campus leader (their rightful position) with all other staff as teacher support. At the same time, it empowered and invited students to be part of the conflict resolution process. After some consideration, the Teacher-Student Mediation Program (TSMP) was born.

The program consisted of two components, the student worksheet and the teacher-staff response and resolution sheet. The front side of the form was called the Student Worksheet and the back the Teacher-

Staff Response. The Student Worksheet asked the receiving student to perform four tasks: explain in their own words what happened; write down what can be done to make things right again; document how he or she would respond in the future to this or similar situations; and write down any questions that they may have for the teacher. On the reverse side of the form, the teacher responds.

After receiving the student's worksheet, the teacher was required to respond in writing and soon thereafter (at a convenient non-classroom instructional time) conduct a mediation conference with the student. The teacher-staff response and resolution sheet addressed the same three points as the student worksheet—infringement recognized, restoration needs, and future expectations. However, the teacher-staff response went a step further. Because the TSMP form was directed back to the teacher of origin, it cast the teacher in a new role. They became the leader in the process. The administration was cast in the role of teacher support; their primary task became stewardship over the integrity of the process.

After leading the student through the process, if an agreement and resolution was reached, the document was signed and the episode closed. If the conflict did not reach a satisfactory conclusion, the teacher or student could ask for additional support. The teacher-staff side of the form also included a question of whether more clarification was needed. If no further discussion was needed, the student and the teacher signed the document and celebrated the resolution. If additional discussion was needed, the restorative circle widened to include an administrator. The TSMP form was more than just a student worksheet and teacher response sheet. It was also designed to be a thought organizer for the student, a discussion guide for the teacher, a contractual agreement, and documentation of the incident.

In the early stages of implementation, the new program was put to the test. I could not have designed a better evaluation scenario. The incident simultaneously tested the process and solidified the staff's belief in its validity.

A black female student became angry in class and called a white male teacher every derogatory term she could dream up. She then stormed out of the classroom. On her way to my office, the student called home and left an inflammatory message for her mother.

When the young lady arrived, I immediately provided her with a TSMP student worksheet. (By the way, according to California Education Code, prior to a suspension the students must be given an opportunity to provide a statement of their version of the incident. They should also be afforded an investigation, including an option to call witnesses. Whether a student is suspended or not, the TSMP provides them a way to be heard in all incidents.) After she completed the worksheet, I returned it to the teacher. Before he had finished his part of the process, the mother arrived on campus.

In the reception area, she was breathing fire and demanding to speak with the principal. The commotion was so loud that I could hear it from my office, which was on the other end of the hallway, more than 100 feet from the reception area. After unsuccessful attempts to calm the parent, Mr. Mitchell brought her to my office to find out what I knew about the situation. The student was still with me awaiting her suspension notification for the profanity. When her mom walked in, the student went from calmly sitting and waiting to putting on a show, or as my mama would call it, "showing her ass." She began to cry and carry on as if she were in the throes of a severe beating by the police. The student's behavior elevated the parent's emotional level to new heights. She then demanded to see the teacher. The teacher was teaching a class at the time, so I suggested that we retrieve the TSMP for review first.

After the mother read the form, she appeared embarrassed. The student had explained the incident in detail and had even admitted she had been profane. (She also cited the exact vulgar language she had used in class.) The form completely recast the incident. The mother humbly apologized to us and said it appeared her daughter had a serious problem, which she would handle at home. She no longer desired to speak with the teacher, and she ordered her daughter to the car. When the student returned from her suspension, before she returned to the teacher's class, they met for mediation. They came to an agreement, and I heard nothing more from either of them for the remainder of the year.

As discussed earlier, the process turned out to be a great way to control the climate of safety in the classroom while preserving the culture of learning. It also laid the foundation for resolving an issue at a more opportune time. In addition, it created instant documentation for noteworthy incidents and served as a basis for authentic relationship building. For those teachers who had difficulty knowing how to approach the discussion, it was as simple as following the outline.

In the final analysis, the teachers accepted the program, and the results were impressive. I knew the process was working well when teachers started coming to me and asking for the mediation sheets instead of the standard referrals. I don't recall exactly when it occurred, but at some point, the traditional referral system was scrapped and TSMP forms were placed in every teacher's mailbox as our officially preferred process.

I was further encouraged when Mr. Littig, a math teacher, told me that after mediation with one of his students, he realized the student was correct. (Remember, the process works both ways. In the mediation meeting, it could easily be determined the student assessment is the more correct one.) What happens then? Mr. Littig got it right. He said he apologized, and their relationship was changed forever. A few years later, while doing an administrator's walk through at Kearney High School in San Diego, the principal said we would be doing an observation of an exemplary teacher. When we walked into the classroom, the teacher was Mr. Littig. We shook hands and hugged. As I looked around the room, I noticed that he displayed many of the posters and materials I had created years earlier while at Gompers. Although his school had not officially adopted the process, he had decided to implement it on an individual basis.

So, let's take a closer look at the Teacher-Student Mediation Program procedure.

There are four parts to the teacher-student mediation program. The parts are as follows:

1. A process introduction to the program
2. Program key accords—ground rules, apologies, and promises
3. An understanding of conflict—the unmanaged cycle and four ways of handling conflict
4. The TSMP form and its usage

- Process Introduction

The TSMP program introduction sheet is the first piece of program literature that should be presented. The introduction sheet should orient everyone to the program's instructional content, goal, and purpose. This orientation task can be accomplished in as little as one page. In fact, I would recommend the program introduction consist of one or two pages at most.

The inspiration for the program— Restorative Justice (RJ) and the Victim Offender Reconciliation Program (VORP)— should be explained. In other words, a brief history of how the principles of RJ and VORP were embodied in the TSMP should be provided. Emphasis should also be placed on an understanding of how the process implementation is designed to improve the climate of safety and culture of learning at school. The introduction should go on to explain what is

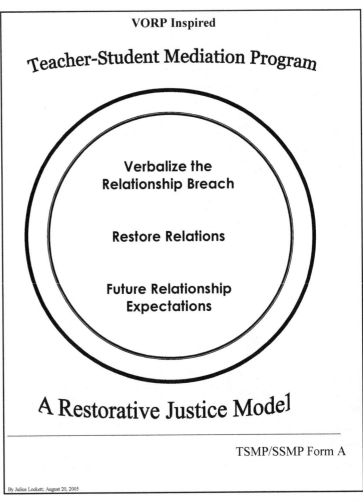

meant by the three goals of the TSMP process— verbalization of the relationship breach, restoring the relationship, and future relationship expectations. A sample introduction sheet follows.

After the introduction, the mediation program key accords must be established.

- **Key Accords**

Key accords include the establishment of ground rules and an opportunity and venue for apologies and promises. There are only two prerequisites for ground rules—clarity and confidentiality. The ground rules must be clearly stated. They must also be explained and discussed prior to beginning any mediation. A sample ground rule document is included in this section. Beyond explaining the ground rules, the confidential nature of the mediation should be confirmed. If the mediation is between a teacher and student, the teacher must make every effort to have the student verbally and physically confirm the expectation of confidentiality. Ideally the mediator would solicit a response something like this, "I understand the confidential nature of the process." In addition, a physical nod of confirmation should be sought. Both gestures—verbal and physical—go a long way towards an open, honest dialogue and an authentic relationship.

During the mediation, beyond recognizing, restoring, and discussing future expectations, time should be allocated for verbal apologies and promises. Apologies and promises can be infused into all three phases of the mediation: the recognition, restoration, and future expectations. Specifically, in the restoration, or making-it-right phase, an apology might be a key element in moving forward. Furthermore, when discussing future expectations, specific promises need to be spelled out. Future expectations language might sound like this: *"Sarah, you are making me a promise to talk and socialize with friends only during instructional transition times. You are also promising to begin assignment activities promptly."* A sample mediation key accords sheet follows.

URBAN ESSENTIALS 101
Unleashing the Academic Potential in Urban Schools

Mediation Key Accords:

Ground Rules

- Be clear about the ground rules. (Example: Be Positive, No Profanity or Aggression)
- Assure and Maintain Confidentiality

Apologies

- Provide an opportunity to apologize
- Document the apologies and/or the opportunity to apologize

Promises

- Clearly document the behavior expectations and future promises

SPECIFIC GROUND RULES for MEDIATION

- We agree to maintain full confidentiality about our participation in this process
- We agree to actively participate in the mediation discussion and resolution process
- We agree to be positive and respectful
- We agree to address the current issue, and to not attack the character of the other participants
- We agree to have an honest conversation and to refrain from distractions like sarcasm, profanity and other obscenities.

· **Understanding Conflict**

Next comes an understanding of conflict. This includes an understanding of the Unmanaged Conflict Cycle and The Four Ways of Handling Conflict.

The Unmanaged Conflict Cycle is used to illustrate for students the psychological components and nature of conflict. It also provides insight and instruction on how to change the cycle. In addition, it may be used to encourage students to buy into the mediation process. The unmanaged conflict cycle graphic is a great teaching tool for students who are more visual and/or logical sequential thinkers. It helps them to understand what they are experiencing and why they continue to repeat the cycle. With this in mind, after the introduction to the mediation process and laying out the key accords, the five steps of the unmanaged conflict cycle are reviewed. The steps include anxiety or tension, uncertainty or role dilemma, inequity tallying or injustice collection, altercation or confrontation, and modifications or adjustments. When the sequence has been thoroughly discussed, I stress the urgency and importance of breaking the cycle and developing healthy relationships.

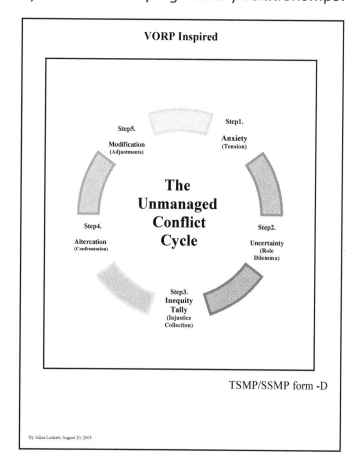

For the sake of time, I will provide only a thumbnail sketch of the unmanaged conflict cycle. In the initial phase of any conflict, there is always anxiety or tension. Once in the anxiety or tension phase, role dilemma or uncertainty usually follows immediately. In this phase, there is confusion, and logical reasoning begins to dissipate. In role dilemma, one is often left feeling as though their authority or legitimacy is being questioned. Following the uncertainty phase comes inequity tallying or injustice collecting. In this phase, all the past wrongs are recalled and calculated. Acting upon the assumed disrespect and infringement of the past wrongs, the altercation becomes almost inevitable. After the altercation occurs, whether verbal, physical, or both, there is usually an adjustment or modification phase. The adjustment could be as benign as a warning or as severe as a suspension or expulsion. The important thing to understand at this juncture is that the cycle can be broken. This leads to the four options for handling conflict.

After discussing the unmanaged conflict cycle, the four options for handling conflict are introduced and examined. In option #1, whether real or imagined, one person believes and attempts to act as though they possess all the power. That person may also believe their power can be exercised in a tyrannical fashion and the other individual is powerless to resist. The inherent problem with this approach to conflict is obvious. In the tyrannical situation, the oppressed individual eventually rebels. If this model were being played out on a school campus, the tyrant or "black star" is the same as a bully and the victim is anyone who feels boxed-in or trapped. In some schools, this may include the teachers. When the rebellion arises, the problem is we never know what form it may take. The oppressed may become a frequent truant or in a worst case scenario, the school shooter. Of course, option #1 is the worst choice for handling conflict.

Option #2 is a better alternative. In this option, all power is surrendered to an outside authority or source. In the public sector, this outside source is often the police and then a judge. In the school setting, it could be the campus police, a counselor, or an administrator. While option #2 is slightly superior to option #1, it often victimizes both participants.

Option #3 is a much better choice. Option #3 is the handling of infringements through a mediator. The difference between option #2 and #3 is that power is initially left in the hands of the actual participants. The mediator is present as a facilitator in the process. This is the option employed in the student-to-student mediation process.

Option #4 is the best way to manage conflict. We refer to this option as a teacher-staff led collaborative mediation. Collaborative mediation allows both parties to equitably share the power and responsibility for resolving their conflict without engaging the other 3 options. This is the model from which the TSMP draws its impetus. After explaining the four options for handling conflict, students are usually able to identify the best option. When given the information and a choice, they readily choose this option. See the graphic that follows.

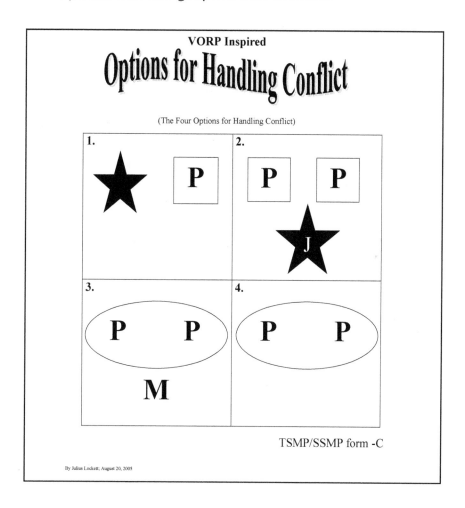

- **The TSMP Form**

After the process introduction, the key accords, and the understanding of conflict, the application of the TSMP form begins. As stated, in California, according to Education Code, each student must be provided an opportunity to make a statement prior to suspension. The TSMP goes a step further; it allows students to make a statement for every incident that occurs. This not only satisfies the state requirement, it also supports relationship building through fairness and inclusiveness.

As mentioned, in the teacher-student model, the teacher simultaneously acts as a participant in, and mediator of, the incident. Because of this delicate dual function, it is crucial for the teacher to fully understand and embrace the mediation process and purpose. With so much at stake, it is easy to see the benefits and necessity of having high quality professional development and training procedures in the mediation process.

As with the VORP model discussed earlier, the goal of the TSMP model is also threefold: 1) to allow the teacher and student an opportunity to verbalize the relationship breach; 2) to discuss ways to make things right again by restoring and repairing the relationship; and 3) to lay out a clear path and plan for their future relationship expectations. A clear contrast should be drawn between the restorative justice system and our current school discipline model, the criminal justice system. The criminal justice model attempts to resolve school disciplinary issues by establishing that an Education Code violation has occurred. It then sets out to identify and punish the student perpetrator. The TSMP model, on the other hand, does not begin its quest by attempting to establish that an Education Code violation has occurred, and it does not attempt to locate and punish students as perpetrators. Instead, it seeks to identify and rectify the harm, then restore the breached relationship. The insert that follows highlights the differences between the criminal justice and restorative justice models:

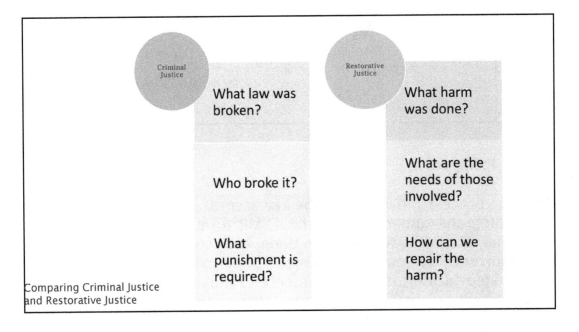

Comparing Criminal Justice and Restorative Justice

When a significant infringement that could not be resolved through a simple warning has occurred, the teacher issues the student an incident worksheet. If the student accepts the form with relative composure, s/he should be allowed to complete the worksheet in the confines of the classroom. If not, the student should be sent to the dean of students, the in-school suspension classroom teacher, assistant/vice principal, or the designated mediation specialist to complete the form.

The student side of the form should include at least three data entry sections—teacher, student, and administrator or designee. On the front of the student worksheet, there should be a quick reference section that allows the teacher to mark or check a box indicating whether they want the student to return immediately upon completion of the form. The reason for this quick reference is simple. It ensures that the teacher is directing the process. If the teacher checks yes, indicating they would like the student to return to class, the in-school suspension classroom teacher will know to expedite the return process. For example, if the student is going to the in-school suspension classroom to merely turn in an electronic device, the in-school suspension classroom teacher will know to secure the device and allow the student to complete the TSMP form, and then promptly send him or her back to class. On the other hand, if the teacher marks no (or neither), the in-school suspension classroom teacher will assume the infringement is perhaps more serious and will act accordingly.

In the student section, there are three primary inquiries made to the student. First, the student is asked to explain the incident from their perspective. Second, the student is asked to offer suggestions for resolving the issue. And third, the student is asked to communicate how they intend to behave once the incident has been resolved. There should also be space allocated for the student to ask the teacher clarifying questions about the incident. The clarifying questions section is there for two reasons. Reason one: it empowers the student by assuring them that their concerns will be heard and addressed.
Reason two: the clarifying questions give the teacher an advance understanding of the student's concerns and ample time for a thoughtful response.

Lastly, the student worksheet side of the form should contain an area for administrator or staff notes. In the staff notes section, the administrator or administrative designee can provide a brief explanation of the processing of the incident. For example, the in-school suspension classroom teacher might say, "The student turned in her cell phone, the incident worksheet was completed, and she was sent back to class at 8:40 AM." Or, "After completing the worksheet, upon request, the student was referred to the counseling office." When the student has finished the worksheet and the administrator or designee has entered processing notes, the form is routed back to the teacher for a response and mediated resolution. This system frees the teacher from the burden of stopping class in order to write a student referral to the administrator. A sample TSMP student worksheet form follows:

There are many ways to construct the TSMP form. The next graphic illustrates a form design used by Kingwoods K-8 in the San Juan Unified School District. Not only did they use their form to recognize, restore, and identify future expectations, they also infused their posture called Give Me 5, directly into the form as part of their standard procedure. On this form, the student is given an opportunity to identify which fundamental posture principle they potentially violated.

Because they are a kindergarten to eighth grade (K-8) school, they took an additional, more therapeutic step. They used their student worksheet side to assess a student's emotional well-being. They inquired about the student's emotions and feelings at the time of the incident. To assist the students in connecting with their feelings, the school provided students with a list of feeling words to draw from. Their list of feelings words is also attached.

KINGSWOOD STUDENT INCIDENT WORKSHEET

Name _____ ID# _____

Date _____ Period_____

Teacher: _____
Send student back this period?
Check one: Yes ☐ No ☐

What "Give Me 5" principle was not followed?

"Be Safe"   "Be Respectful"   "Be Responsible"   "Be Here"   "Be Ready to Learn"

In your own words, explain what happened

List any emotions you were feeling at the moment of the incident (look at the list of feelings):

List any questions that you may have about the conflict/incident.
(Remember, questions begin with Who, What, When, Where, Why, How, Did and other interrogatories.)

1.	3.
2.	4.

What would make things right again, Right Now?

If things are made as right as possible, how will you deal with this person or situation in the future?

Administrator/Staff Notes:

TSMP/SSMP form -E

Children's List of Feeling Words:

GLAD	SAD	MAD	AFRAID	OTHER
content		bugged	uncomfortable	shy
glad	blah	annoyed	startled	curious
pleased	blue	irritated	uneasy	sassy
playful	gloomy	mean	tense	weird
cheerful	rotten	crabby	anxious	confused
giddy	sad	cranky	worried	moody
calm	unhappy	grumpy	concerned	small
comfortable	empty	grouchy	timid	quiet
cozy				jealous
safe		_____	_____	embarrassed*
relaxed	_____	_____	_____	guilty*
confident*	_____			responsible**
strong				concerned**
peaceful				ashamed*
				caring**
_____				bored
_____				
				_____
delighted	disappointed	disgusted	alarmed	_____
jolly	hurt	ticked off	scared	
bubbly	lost	mad	afraid	
tickled	sorry	angry	frightened	
silly	ashamed	smoldering	fearful	
frisky	lonely	hot	threatened	
happy	down	frustrated	trembly	
proud*	hopeless	impatient	shaken	
joyful	discouraged		disturbed	
excited	awful	_____		
thankful		_____	_____	
great	_____		_____	
loved/loving	_____			
blissful				
grateful**				
satisfied				
_____				
_____				
alive	miserable	fed-up	dread	
sparkly	crushed	fuming	panicky	
wonderful	helpless	infuriated	terrified	
ecstatic	depressed	destructive	horrified	
terrific	withdrawn	explosive	petrified	
jubilant	heartbroken	violent		
	unloved	enraged	_____	
_____		furious	_____	
	_____			
	_____	_____		
		_____		

*self-conscious emotions-
**empathic emotions-

When a teacher receives a student worksheet, the mediation response process is triggered. This response process requires the teacher to complete the reverse side of the student worksheet. The teacher side of the form is referred to as the Teacher-Staff Response and Resolution. The teacher (or any staff member) must first read and consider the student's worksheet. (The currently-used school referral process, which only allows for a statement from the teacher, has been part of the problem in urban underserved schools in part because it did not allow for a mutual interchange. The ability to be heard is important for all students. It is a seriously held value among urban underserved students.)

Therefore, after considering the student's worksheet, the teacher completes their side of the form. The teacher's response form is also a three-pronged response. The sheet includes sections that afford the teacher an opportunity to explain the incident from their perspective—facts and feelings—and then lay out an unambiguous strategy, which may include consequences for making things right again. I must make a point here about making things right from the teacher's perspective. I feel this section of the form is the most significant part of the entire process. In this section, teachers are placed in a position of nearly complete authority and discretion. They are asked to outline the potential consequences. Nowhere in the criminal justice based referral system are teachers afforded an opportunity to do this. I would be remiss if I did not tell the following story associated with the nature and understanding of this section.

When we first implemented this process at Gompers Secondary School in San Diego, one of the veteran teachers brought her TSMP to my office for a process discussion. The student had completed their half, and, after reading it, the teacher wanted to know what I intended to do about it. Since she had not completed her half of the form, I sat with her and we worked through it together. When we got to the part that asked the question "Making things right again will require the following measures," she was at a loss. So, I asked her what consequences she would like to make things right again. She looked at me and said, "You are the administrator, don't you know what should be done?" I laughed, and said "I know what I would want done under the circumstances." I went on to explain the question was asking her what she wanted done. It then dawned on me that she and many other teachers were unaccustomed to making disciplinary decisions about the students. It made complete sense. They were accustomed to sending students away for this, so they never had to think about what they desired. This fundamental understanding helped me to be more helpful to teachers.

I believe most teachers have no real conception of corrective consequences. I also believe that in many cases teachers fail to understand that when they send a student away for disciplinary consequences it actually erodes their authority and discretion. On that day, my job became clearer. I recognized I had to spend more time helping teachers think about the consequences and outcomes they desired. If their goal was to keep a student in class and learning, I explained it was important for students to respect their authority. I went on to explain how the TSMP process placed discretionary authority directly into their hands. Thereafter, I explained how, once students understood this, respect for their authority would dramatically increase. When the rationale was understood by the teachers, they embraced the discipleship process far better than I could have ever imagined. It is vital for the teacher to understand clearly and communicate specifically the consequences needed to make things right again. After understanding the value of making things right, instead of suspension the teacher opted for an apology and a promise to correct behavior. In a follow up discussion, the teacher expressed that the mediation had gone well. Thereafter, that teacher became something of an ambassador for the process.

The final entry for the teacher revolves around the future expectations. Future expectations are an instrumental feature for sustaining a viable relationship when the student has been reunited with the class. Clear expectations are paramount. An easy way to approach your future expectations is to tie them back to the school's fixed inputs—the posture, rules, expectations and BIP.

Once the teacher has completed the response form, it is mandatory for the student to attend a teacher-led mediation conference. The conference should be held after school and should not be treated as detention or punishment. Instead, it should be viewed as a venue for discussion, resolution, and relationship building.

The conference is the perfect setting for getting to know the student on a more personal level. After a resolution has been reached, a positive discussion around academic needs or behavior observations might be discussed as possible insights and indicators leading to conflict. It is also an ideal time to secure useful, updated data like new telephone contact numbers for parents and guardians. For the most part, however, the venue should be maintained as a safe and welcoming environment for mediating and resolving the conflict at hand.

If all issues are resolved in the conference, the teacher and the student will sign the agreement section of the Teacher Response Sheet and the completed process becomes a documented contract. However, if there are other issues that require further discussion, either party may request an expansion of the restorative circle to include an administrator. If the issue is still not resolved, the restorative circle could widen even more. It might include the parent, other teachers, and even other students if agreed upon. When all positions are satisfied, the resolution agreement document must be endorsed. (Although it is not mandatory, a copy of the completed document may be issued to the student.)

The documented contract is the overt indication that the process has been completed and the issue resolved. At this point, the completed document begins to serve several other functions. In addition to being a resolution agreement and contract, the completed document is a viable means of recordkeeping. If needed, the document may also serve as evidence for Education Code compliance and a key component of a comprehensive school site intervention strategy process. Nonetheless, as stated, the primary purpose of the document is evidence that an agreement has been reached, the incident has been resolved, and a stronger relationship has been built. A sample Teacher Staff Response and Resolution sheet follows.

Teacher / Staff Response and Resolution

Responder _____ Date _____

Student _____ Incident Date _____

In reply to your correspondence:

Facts (what happened, response to questions, etc.):

Making things right again will require the following measures:

My future expectations are as follows:

Is more discussion needed?   Yes ☐   No ☐

(If additional support is needed, the process will be transferred to the designated administrator.)

If all positions are now clarified, please endorse below.

Signatures and Celebration of Agreement

_____ Date _____

_____ Date _____

Witness _____ Date _____

Witness _____ Date _____

TSMP form -F

© Julius Lockett, August 20, 2005

- ## The TSMP 12-step mediation process

Recognizing that some teachers and staff may need a conversational guide or outline for the mediation meeting, we at UE101 created a 12-step model for teacher-student mediation. This effort was led by Alison Wohlgemuth, a long time UE101 associate and Director of Discovering the Reality of our Community (D.R.O.C.) of Bay Area Community Resources in Richmond, California. The graphic that follows illustrates the UE101 recommended mediation process. When a student arrives for mediation, inexperienced teachers may simply follow the process guideline.

THE UE101 MEDIATION PROCESS
Recognize the Breach + Restore the Relationship + Make it Right for the Future

1. Give thanks	7. Recognize the student's words on making it right now and in the future
2. State the reason for meeting	8. Share what will make it right for you, right now
3. State the ground rules	9. Describe explicit instructions for future behavior expectations
4. Acknowledge the student's story	10. Agree on future behavior
5. Share the behaviors you observed	11. Sign the agreement
6. Address the student's questions	12. Celebrate the Resolution

... The Student-Student Mediation Program (SSMP)

As stated earlier, the student-student mediation program (SSMP) was the first implementation created by UE101. The SSMP is a more traditional mediation practice. In the four ways of handling conflict graphic, the SSMP aligns with method number three. It involves two or more students and a skilled mediator. Although I will not speak in depth about the SSMP process in this book, the technique and practice is a vital part of the overall climate management arsenal at urban underserved schools. Ideally, the SSMP should be employed whenever there is significant student conflict. It is also the process undertaken when two students return to school after being suspended for fighting or some more serious interaction.

In the best-case scenario, the mediator of an SSMP should be a counselor, the in-school suspension classroom teacher, dean of students, vice principal, principal, or a trusted designee. Regardless of the selection, it is imperative that the individuals be trained in mediation by a reliable restorative justice organization. The experience and training should be in the areas of mediation, conflict management, and the art and science of creating a positive school climate and culture.

The mediator's responsibility in the intervention is to lead the students through the process of healing and restoration in a manner that is safe and inspiring for all involved. Using the program's education forms—the program introduction sheet, the unmanaged conflict cycle, and the four options for handling conflict sheet—the mediator, just as in the TSMP, should educate the students on the injurious nature of the experience and the necessity for the mediation resolution process. The first thing that must occur is the building of trust between the mediator and the students involved. This is accomplished by the mediator as he or she declares their neutrality—or better still, actively asserts their concern for the welfare of all participants. Also, the laying out of the key accords—ground rules, apologies and promises—will contribute to the sense of trust and safety. After the issue of safety and trust has been addressed and established, the mediator is ready to formally introduce the participants to the process materials.

· **The Program Introduction Sheet**

Only the SSMP program introduction sheet will be discussed here, as it differs slightly from TSMP program introduction sheet. The other forms—the unmanaged conflict cycle, four ways of handling conflict, and the key accords—are the same forms presented in the discussion of the TSMP.

Just as with the TSMP, the SSMP program introduction sheet is the first piece of program literature given to the participants. The introduction sheet should explain the purpose and goal of the program. This program introduction task can and should be accomplished in as few as one or two pages. The orientation should not take more than five or ten minutes to complete.

The goal and purpose of the SSMP, like the TSMP, RJ and VORP is threefold: to verbalize the relationship breach, restore the failed relationship, and lay out a clear path and plan for future relationship expectations. The introduction sheet should also make it clear that the program model is restorative justice as opposed to criminal justice. In urban underserved schools, and perhaps in schools in general, most students interpret a process that involves adults as punitive in nature and part of the criminal justice model. Consequently, they are often reticent, skeptical, and even hostile about participation. Therefore, it is critical for the students to know you are not seeking to identify and punish a perpetrator, but you are seeking to restore their relationships and lay the foundation for more positive future exchanges. An SSMP program introduction sheet graphic follows:

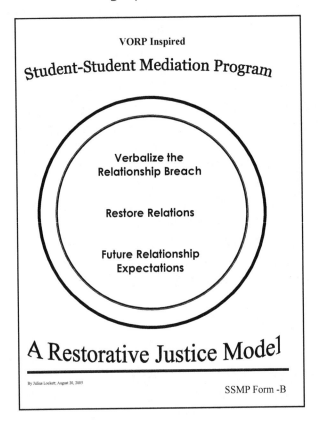

• **The Student Incident Worksheet**

When the program introduction has been completed, the mediation process begins. As a way of streamlining the process as well as creating continuity and familiarity, the student form used in the SSMP is the same form as used in the TSMP. The only difference is in the implementation of the process. In the SSMP, the students involved in the conflict complete the worksheet section by section with the mediator functioning as facilitator and guide. A sample SSMP form follows:

**UEHS STUDENT – STUDENT
INCIDENT WORKSHEET**

Name _____ Incident Date _____ Time / Period _____ AM/PM

In your own words, explain what happened

List any questions that you may have about the conflict/incident.
(Remember, questions begin with Who, What, When, Where, Why, How, Did and other interrogatories.)

1.	3.
2.	4.

What would make things right again?

If things are made as right as possible, how will you deal with this person or situation in the future?

Administrator/Staff Notes:

By Julius Lockett; August 20, 2005

TSMP/SSMP form -E

As facilitator, the mediator's role is to ensure that each element—verbalizing the relationship breach, restoring relations, and agreeing on future relationship expectations—is equitably, fairly and thoroughly fleshed out in a respectful and positive manner, while assisting the students in the development of an unbiased and reasonable resolution. When the process begins, each student is asked to jot down in bullet form their interpretation of the incident. When the students are finished writing, each is given an opportunity to articulate their interpretation of the breach without interruption. While the first student explains what happened, the responsibility of the other student is to listen and write down any questions they might have regarding the other student's account. When the first student is done, the other student is given an opportunity to ask any clarifying questions they might have. When the questioning is completed, the process is repeated. The second student explains the incident while the other student listens and jots down clarifying questions. When the explanations and clarifying questions have been exhausted, the mediation moves into the next phase. In this phase the question becomes, "What would make things right again?"

Each student is asked to reflect on the other student's understanding of the incident, consider the information and discussion, then write down what would make things right between them. This is an ideal time to reintroduce the key accords of apologies and promises as part of restoration. When the students have submitted their proposals, it is the mediator's role and responsibility to merge the two sets of needs into a cohesive list.

After a mutual agreement has been reached as it relates to making things right again, the third and final phase—future expectations—will be introduced. In this phase, both students will be asked to write down their expectation for future interaction. This is an ideal time and place for promises to be made. For ease of information consolidation and the drafting of the final agreement, the making it right phase and future intentions phase of the mediation will be documented by the mediator on the Resolution Worksheet: Making it Right and Future Intentions form. A copy of the form follows:

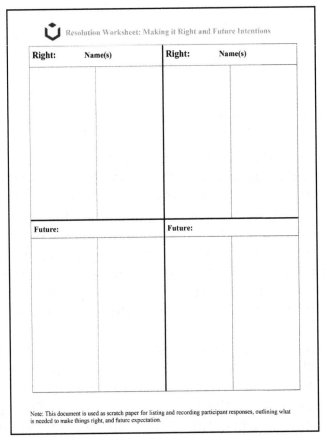

- The Resolution and Agreement Form

The pinnacle of success in an SSMP is a just, equitable, and fair resolution and agreement. The agreement should contain a brief explanation of the mediation proceedings and how the conflict was resolved. There should also be a section that clearly sets the framework for future interaction. The document must also contain a section dedicated to the affixing of signatures, including all participants—students, mediator and, if applicable, witnesses.

A copy of the finished document should be issued to each participant. In addition, a file folder, consisting of the used worksheets and the original agreement, should be created and maintained for future reference.
The resolution and agreement document serves four basic functions. First and foremost, the agreement serves as a relationship builder. It is documentation that a formalized reconciliatory resolution between the students was reached. The document also serves as certification that a school-directed comprehensive intervention process strategy was pursued. Next, the completed file and agreement serves as a visible means of incident documentation and record keeping. Finally, if needed, the resolution agreement serves as a criminal justice crossover evidentiary document. A blank and a completed sample of the UE101 Resolution and Agreement form follows:

RESOLUTION & AGREEMENT

The Persons Listed Have Recognized And Resolved Their Differences.

Print Names(s): _____

_____

_____

_____

Things were made right by taking the following measures:

In the future, we agree to do the following:

Signatures and Celebrations

_____ Date _____

_____ Date _____

Witness _____ Date _____

Witness _____ Date _____

By Julius Lockett; August 20, 2005

SSMP form -G

RESOLUTION & AGREEMENT

The Persons Listed Have Recognized And Resolved Their Differences.

Print Names(s):   Shontae Greer

_____
Wesley Green

_____

_____

Things were made right by taking the following measures:

| We were given an opportunity to explain what happened in our own words. We were also |
| allowed to ask and answer questions about the incident. Shontae apologized for not giving |

| Wesley an opportunity to explain what happen before he pushed him. Wesley accepted the |
| apology. Shontae also agreed to reimburse Wesley $24.00 for the cost of his ripped shirt. |

| Wesley also apologized to Shontae for any disrespectful looks in the past. Shontae accepted |

| Wesley's apology. |

In the future, we agree to do the following:

| We will respect each other. That means, we will not fight, and we will acknowledge each other in a |
| friendly, positive way when passing. Shontae promises to approach Wesley in a calm way and use a |
| positve tone if he has questions about comments that he might have heard. Wesley agreed |
| to do likewise. Both students promise to govern themselves using the STRIVE posture in the future. If |
| there is an incident that either feels is to serious to go to the other, it will be brought to the ISSCT or DOS. |

Signatures and Celebrations

Shontae Greer _____ Date 11/19/2014

Wesley Green _____ Date 11/19/2014

Witness _Sarah Scott, DOS_ _____ Date 11/19/2014

Witness _____ Date _____

By Julius Lockett; August 20, 2005

SSMP form -G

- ## The SSMP 12-step mediation process

Recognizing that some staff members may need a conversational guideline for mediation, we at UE101 created a 12-step mediation process for the SSMP. This is the final detail mechanism I will offer as it relates to the conducting of student to student mediation. The graphic that follows illustrates the UE101 SSMP mediation process.

The UE101 Student – Student Mediation Process	
Recognize the Breach + Restore the Relationship + Make it Right for the Future	
1. Give thanks	7. Write and Clarify the making it right process
2. State the reason for meeting	8. Lead Students in the future relationship process
3. Share the ground rules	9. Write and clarify the resolution agreement
4. Allow the students to write and share their account of the incident	10. Sign the Agreement
5. Allow the students to ask questions	11. Allow for verbalized final thoughts
6. Lead Students in the making it right process	12. Celebrate the agreement

... The (New) In-School Suspension Classroom Program (ISSC)

The ISSC Program is a critical and integral implementation for the success of your school improvement plan. The program is so significant that it should no longer be called in-school suspension, as it is not by any means your grandfather's version of in-school suspension. This program is not about isolation and punishment. It is about inspiration and instruction. It is the intervention nexus of communication between all school affiliates. Therefore, to cast the program in a slightly more favorable light, think of it as the New ISSC Program. As you read further, you will understand why it is an improvement. Let's start with an understanding about in-school suspension in California.

In California, in-school suspension is identified as an alternative to home suspension. It is a mechanism that California Education Code is relatively clear on and straightforward about. It is defined in code section 48911.1. In subsection (a) of the code, it asserts that a student may be assigned to a "supervised suspension classroom for the entire period of [a] suspension . . . ."[47] Then in subsections (b) and (c) the code goes on to provide the stipulations for utilizing this intervention. The stipulation even includes whether a school will be financially compensated for students assigned an in-school suspension.

Schools run on money and, in California, when a student is absent or under suspension, no money is paid for that day. The money paid for each day is called ADA or Average Daily Attendance. If a student is in the ISSC, a school may claim the money as though the student were present for a regular school day.[48] To claim the money, there are five conditions that must be met. The first condition is intended for campus safety. It requires that suspended students be separated from the general population. The other conditions are designed more for student enrichment. The ISSC must be "staffed as otherwise provided by law." That means a state certificated classroom teacher. The participating students must have access to appropriate counseling services. The program should also promote the completion of missing schoolwork and tests missed while on suspension. The student has the responsibility of contacting the teacher for the work, and the teacher has a responsibility to provide the work. The final directive for in-school suspension is parent notification. If a student is placed on in-school suspension, the Education Code requires a parent or guardian be notified in person or by telephone. If a student is placed on ISSC for more than one period, the notification should be in writing. This can easily be accomplished via email.

The Education Code surrounding the ISSC is perfect for our "new" program development. The mandate requiring the teacher to provide assignments is my favorite stipulation in the statute, not because it places an additional burden on teachers but for a far more practical reason. In the statute it indeed states that the teacher shall provide assignments, but it then it then goes on to say that "if no classroom work is assigned, the person supervising the suspension classroom shall assign schoolwork." That one clause is a bonanza for potential school improvement. And it is upon that single clause that we base the

New ISSC Program.

In the past, I have had the opportunity to observe ISSC programs staffed by a liaison (security), counselor, or even their resource officer (police). We do not suggest any of these. The benefit of using such critical staff is marginal and unless they are certificated teachers, it appears to be a violation of Education Code. Besides this, we think we have developed a far more innovative and productive strategy, and the answer was in the Education Code all along.

Here is the direction we at UE101 took with the New ISSC Program. We built a program where every aspect of the Education Code was incorporated to the fullest. Beyond ensuring campus safety through separation, the first and most important aspect of the program design involved the selection of the right In-School Suspension Classroom Teacher (ISSCT).

In the 2009 school year, Keiller Leadership Academy, a charter middle school in San Diego, was the first school to hire an ISSCT using a job description developed in collaboration with UE101 guidelines and values. Prior to the selection, a security liaison with a school counselor credential staffed their ISSC. This was an admirable effort; however, it only touched a portion of the Education Code requirement.

The new job description was developed through a collaborative process between the administration and staff. The following is a summary of the position's requirements along with the necessary candidate qualifications:

The In-School Suspension Classroom Teacher instructs (teaches) and assists ISSC students in completing all classroom assignments, and improved class and campus behavior. In addition, the In-School Suspension Classroom Teacher collaborates with parents, teachers, and administrators to increase the possibility of student achievement.

For a candidate to be eligible for this position, he or she must possess a California Multiple Subject credential or a Single Subject credential with a Supplemental Certification in English, Math, or Science. A candidate must also have experience working with middle-high school students with difficulties in behavior management.

A copy of that job description is inserted in its original form.

In-School Suspension Classroom Teacher
Job Description

Job Title: In-School Suspension Classroom Teacher
Classification: Certificated
Reports To: Principal, or Principal Designee
Prepared Date: April 7, 2010
Approved By:
Approved Date:

SUMMARY: The In-School Suspension Classroom Teacher (ISSCT) instructs (teaches) and assists students, who have been placed in the In-School Suspension Classroom (ISSC) Program, to complete all classroom assignments, and improve class and campus behavior. In addition, the ISSCT collaborates with parents, teachers, and administrators to increase the possibility of student achievement.

ESSENTIAL DUTIES AND RESPONSIBILITIES of the ISSCT include, but are not limited to, the following:

In accordance with California Education Code Section 48911.1, the **[Insert Your District Name]**, and the philosophy of **[Insert Your School Name]**, the ISSCT:

Provides instructional assistance to, and works to build authentic relationships with, students assigned to the ISSC program

Develops a program designed to identify, analyze, act in response, and assess the individual academic and behavioral needs of the ISSC students

In accordance with Ed. Code Sec. 48911.1 (c) (4), plans and teaches lessons as necessary

Insures that all class assignments are completed and routed to the assigning teacher

Maintains appropriate disciplinary behavior in the ISSC

Confers with students individually and/or in groups to modify unacceptable behavior and emphasize positive relationships.

Contacts and confers with parents, as needed

Attends and participates in staff development and training sessions

Consults with teachers daily, and makes appropriate reports regarding student progress and assignments

Works with teachers and counselors to identify students in need of additional assistance from outside community groups or agencies

Clarifies the purpose, goals and policies of the ISSC for teachers, parents and volunteers, Keeps records and completes necessary reports for the program on a timely basis

ISSCT Hire form - A

In-School Suspension Classroom Teacher

QUALIFICATIONS: To perform this job successfully, an individual must be able to perform each essential duty satisfactorily. The requirements listed below are representative of the knowledge, skills, and/or abilities required.

EDUCATION, CERTIFICATES, EXPERIENCE
In order for a candidate to be eligible for this position, he or she must possess a California Multiple Subject credential or a Single Subject credential with a Supplemental Certification in English, Math, or Science. A candidate must also have experience working with middle-high school students with difficulties in behavior management.

COMMUNICATION and TECHNOLOGY SKILLS
A candidate must possess excellent communication skills, and have the ability to formulate and present oral, written, and technology-enhanced visual information. The candidate must be familiar with basic Microsoft Office programs and functions, such as *Word, Excel and PowerPoint*. The candidate must also be willing to learn, use, and instruct others in the use of a lesson plan program—i.e. Plan Book.

ACADEMIC SKILLS
A candidate must possess general education skills in the core subject areas: Math, Science, History, and English. A short qualification exam may be issued.

REASONING ABILITY
A candidate must possess the ability to assess and solve problems associated with teacher, student, and parent relations using a multiplicity of strategies, including arbitration, negotiation, and mediation.

EVALUATION
The performance of this job will be evaluated in accordance with the approved **[Insert Your District Name]** evaluation process for classroom teachers.

ISSCT Hire form - A

The California Education Code made it possible for us to hire a person that was uniquely qualified as an inspirational instructional leader. Beyond the ISSCT, there is another vital aspect: the program itself.

The New ISSC program was developed on two levels, macro and micro. The macro-program consists of three components: Instructional Program Procedures, Inspirational Program Collaboration and a General Education Return Process.

See the graphic that follows for the general component summary.

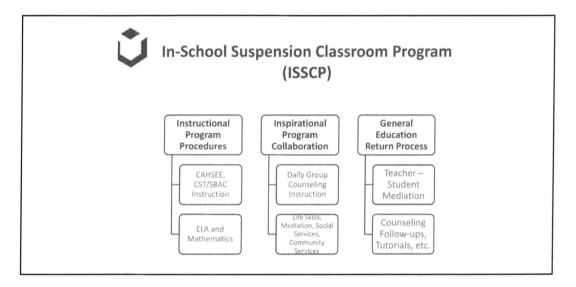

This triad may be further reduced into the New ISSC micro-organizational outline. The graphic that follows is a generalized suggested outline. The final program description will, of course, be determined by the individual district and/or school site.

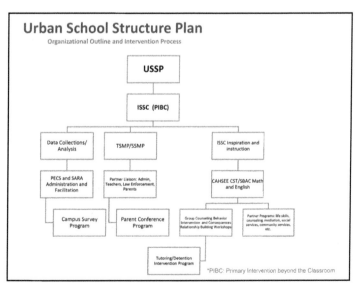

As indicated in the graphic, the ISSC task might include the following components:

1. Data collection and analysis

2. PECS and SARA (to be discussed later) administration and facilitation

3. Campus (climate and culture) Survey program organization and maintenance

4. TSMP/SSMP organization, initiation and storage

5. Partner Liaison: administration, Teacher, Student and Community Affiliates programs

6. Parent Conference Program

7. ISSC Inspiration and instruction

8. CAHSEE and CST and/or SBAC (or the latest testing adoption) Math and English Instruction plan

9. Group Counseling, Behavior Intervention and Consequences, and Relationship Building Workshops

10. Partner Programs: life skills, counseling (intern and/or fieldwork students), mediation, social services, community services and others

11. Tutoring/Library Instruction Hour Intervention program

Now that I have confused and exhausted you, I'll try to simplify it by explaining the process on an application level. So, what does the New ISSC look like, and how does it work?

The basic process is outlined in the following graphic. An additional process guide is provided by Sierra Pacific High School in Hanford, California. They, along with many other schools that implemented the new model, dropped the ISSC label altogether and adopted the new title of Intervention Center or IC. Their IC includes additional features such as an instructional aide for extra assistance.

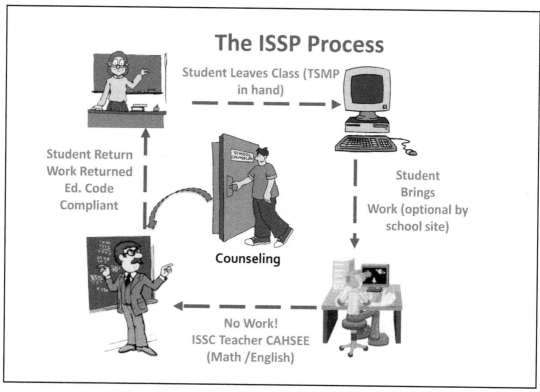

The UE101 New ISSC program model ——————————————

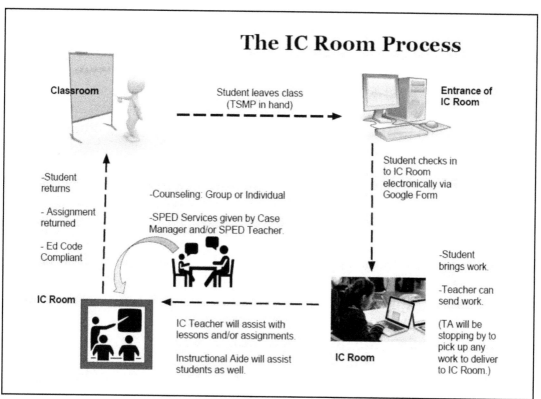

The Sierra Pacific High School Intervention Center Process ——————

Here's how the process works. Whenever a student is asked to leave a classroom, they proceed to the ISSC or IC. The first question that is always asked is what if they don't go? Initially, I jokingly reply that we already know who they are and where they attend school. In other words, we know how to find them and hold them accountable. The real answer to this question is that there is a failsafe mechanism already built into the program. Actually, there are two. First, the TSMP worksheet must be returned to the assigning teacher for mediation. No returned form is an indication that something is amiss. For more immediate feedback, a process was created by Sarah Morgan, UE101 associate and a school librarian at Campolindo High School in the Acalanes Union High School District. Using google docs, she created a system that automatically sends the teacher an email when the student electronically signs in at the IC.

Once signed in, the student completes the TSMP, and then gets started on the classroom assignment, CAHSEE or CST/SBAC or other test preparation Math or English. Thereafter, if the student happens to be in the IC when the ISSCT's prep period arises, they get a bonus. When the ISSCT leaves, a counselor comes in to lead a group counseling period. The counseling topics are unlimited. They might include anger management, decision making, time management, appropriate responses, school posture, or even the unmanaged conflict cycle. While on the topic of counseling services, just for signing into the IC, the student receives an additional counseling bonus. Every student who signs into the IC gets assigned to a counseling caseload for a follow up meeting with an intern or fieldwork counselor. How does the counseling staff keep up with this new caseload, you might ask? They don't. These caseload counselors may potentially be obtained free of charge from local colleges and universities. Many universities offer counseling Pupil Personnel Services (PPS) credentialing programs. In most cases, these students must complete 600 hours of intern or fieldwork training as part of their credentialing program. This constitutes free services and the possibility of the development of a long-lasting community partnership. Regardless of the nature of the campus or classroom incident, the same process should be followed. If the incident is too serious for the student to go directly to the IC and they must be removed from campus for safety reasons, upon returning from suspension or expulsion, as previously mentioned, the student must reverse the process. While reversing the process, the student will be assigned to a counseling caseload at the IC. Just as a reminder, students are to be sent directly to the principal, vice principal or principal designee's office only for serious infractions like fighting, drugs and so forth.

When the process is all said and done, there is a logical flow that emerges. The process and interventional steps may be as elaborate as the staff feels is necessary. Components may be added or eliminated as necessary. The overall three-part process—Instructional Program Procedures, Inspirational Program Collaboration, and a General Education Return Process—should not be compromised. The flow chart that follows outlines the interventions and process flow.

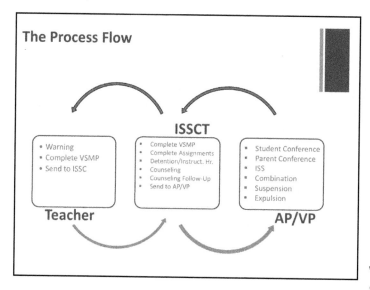

The New ISSC can be a game changer at your school. With proper implementation, behavior problems are dramatically reduced. The data alone gleaned from the IC is worth the effort. If the information is documented and recorded in a database program, a school will be able to glean useful statistics, for example: who are the students going to ISSC; in what period are they going; and what is the reason for going? When the program is fully developed, it is easy to identify and assist the students requiring additional intervention and to automatically trigger the process for providing those services.

... **The Problem, Effect, Cause, and Solution (PECS) and The Survey, Analysis, Response, and Assessment (SARA) Program**

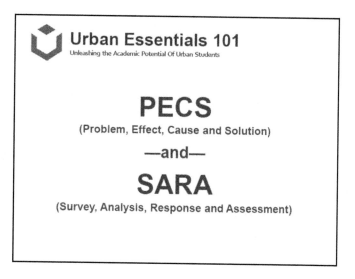

The PECS and SARA Program is a sitewide structural support tool created by UE101. It was developed as a means of identifying and addressing persistent systemic physical plant and safety issues, thus promoting buy-in and creating positive professional relationships among staff members. PECS is an acronym for Problem, Effect, Cause and Solution, while SARA stands for Survey, Analysis, Response and Assessment. In short, PECS identifies and brings campus facilities problems to the forefront, while SARA confirms the issue and offers possible solutions for rectification.

I first learned about the acronym PECS while in the teacher education program at Fresno Pacific University. However, it had nothing to do with maintaining school facilities. In one of my classes, the professor asked that we take a PECS approach in responding to writing prompts and assignments. We were told the process would keep our writings concise, and give us a more professional writing presence, which is highly valued in the education community. Because the FPU teacher education program was quite progressive, the process was most likely developed as a means of responding to prompts for Project Based Learning—a teaching method in which students gain knowledge and skills by working for an extended period to investigate and respond to an engaging and complex question, problem, or challenge.[49]

Using the PECS writing process, we could succinctly identify an alleged problem, explain the presumed effect(s) of its continued existence, declare the assumptive cause, and offer a potential solution. Because I had observed and heard so many complaints being registered about how facilities and maintenance problems never got resolved in schools, I decided that bringing the issue forward to the administration as a PECS might yield better results. I soon learned this was not the case. Bringing a problem forward does not necessarily guarantee a solution. So, what was the answer? SARA!

As stated earlier, prior to entering my career in education, I was a Fulton County (GA) police officer for ten years. In graduate school and while working as a police officer, I learned about the SARA process. It was created in 1987 as a prominent feature of the Community Oriented Policing Model.[50] SARA in the law enforcement realm stands for scanning, analysis, response, and assessment. Designed and used as an investigative tool, it is a strategic way of assessing a criminal complaint to determine its validity and, more importantly, how to best allocate scarce resources to rectify the situation.

One of the best examples of a successful implementation of SARA took place in San Diego, California. The only difference between the SDPD and my usage of the process is in the terminology. Again, in law enforcement the "S" is for Scanning while in the UE101 process the "S" is for surveying. The targeted San Diego SARA site was an apartment complex that had become a haven for crime and drugs. As a result of the continued deterioration, the long-term residents and other community members began to complain vehemently to city officials. It was alleged that non-residents were frequenting the complex day and night, and the bulk of trafficking was taking place near a laundry room. The SARA team set up in an apartment nearby and simply watched and recorded the activity. The surveillance required minimal resource allocation.

After scanning the situation and analyzing the results, it was determined there was a legitimate problem. Shortly thereafter, the team developed and deployed a response. Lastly, they assessed the effectiveness of their efforts. Because of the process, in short order, the problem was eradicated, the complex rejuvenated, and the community and law enforcement relationship improved.

Here is how the school version of PECS and SARA program came into being. I don't recall the exact circumstances, but while working at Gompers Secondary, there was a persistent physical plant problem everyone seemed to know about. The issue was discussed throughout campus as though it had been going on years. And, as I discovered, it had. When I was told of the issue by several different teachers, I assumed its legitimacy. However, I did not accept that nothing could be done. So, I sat down to contemplate what to do. PECS just popped into my mind. I met with a couple of well-known renegade teachers and explained the process. They agreed to complete a PECS form and take our conclusion to the principal.

We could clearly identify the problem, the effect it was having, the presumed cause, and we suggested a potential solution. I thought it all worked out fairly well. The clear need for SARA, however, immediately arose. Although we had skillfully applied PECS to the concern, not much was done thereafter. It was obvious that nothing would occur beyond the problem identification effort. In essence, the PECS just sat and died in an inbox on someone's desk. When I mustered the courage to ask the principal about the missing PECS form, he did not recall seeing it. I decided to tell him there had been an ongoing conversation about the problem and that the teachers believed nothing was going to be done to resolve it. I explained why I thought it was important to resolve, and the principal agreed. We then launched into a PECS hunt. We found the

document on his desk among mountains of paperwork.

I concluded the lack of response to the PECS had nothing to do with the principal's desire to support the effort, nor his presumed laziness. This is my take. In general, administrators are in their positions because they want to be of service, and they simply have a lot on their plates. To the staff members, however, the non-responsiveness or inactivity may feel like an affront or, in the worst-case scenario, ineptness or laziness. In most cases I think it is none of these. I think the answer is most administrators are overwhelmed by the work, and thus they prioritize. I further believe that unless the concern is an immediate or extreme hazard or a demand from district superiors, it takes a back seat. In reality, the typical administrator's work is often about fighting the immediate fire.

When problems don't seem to get resolved, staff members feel it's just another unfulfilled promise, and it erodes staff confidence in the administration's desire and/or leadership. SARA, therefore, was just a logical addition. By applying SARA, it all but guaranteed a response to the PECS without the proverbial languishing on the desk. I told the principal about the potential benefits of using the SARA process and he agreed to give it a try.

The next time the program was used, we incorporated both. SARA sealed the deal. I am now blessed with so many examples of this duo working wonders. For the sake of time and space, I will offer only one. It was all about the birds.

At Morse High School in San Diego, there was a hovering problem— birds. The school was on the lunch itinerary of a flock of seagulls. Like clockwork, when lunch ended, the birds swooped in for a leftover food fest. Like a plethora of Pavlovian poultry, when the bell rang, they encircled the lunch court and dive-bombed the courtyard. It was pure pandemonium! Birds were cackling and pooping, students screaming and running, teachers ducking, glaring and complaining, and administrators yelling for the students to stop running, while dashing about with trash pickup tools trying to best the seagulls. When I first saw the scene being played out, it was comical— until a teacher told me the problem had been going on for years.

I asked the principal if we could try to resolve the issue with PECS and SARA, and he enthusiastically agreed. A couple teachers agreed to write it up, and others agreed to form a SARA team to assist in resolving the matter. It worked perfectly.

The PECS was written in a fairly humorous manner:

The Problem—being terrorized from the sky
Effect—safety and sanitation
Cause—out of control, disrespectful students throwing trash everywhere
Solution—suspending students for littering, and hiring administrators with backbones!

The PECS, with the possible exception of the Solution, sounded fairly plausible, but the SARA team threw a bit of a wrench in the situation. While the SARA team conceded that the problem and effect had merit, they didn't see the cause and solution from the same perspective.

Here is the SARA team's reaction:

Survey—a few teachers with clipboards watched and took notes from strategic positions around the lunch court. We also asked some students why they left their trash behind.

Analysis— we agree there is a problem and the potential effects are confirmed. After observing the area and speaking with several students, we have determined the problem to be too few trash cans. As the available cans quickly filled up, the students just started throwing the trash near the cans. Further, many of the students stated that they were leaving the trash on the ground, tables and in other areas because from their locations, they could see the full trash cans and simply decided to leave it behind. There appeared to be minimal deliberate littering.

Response—the team recommends doubling the number of trash cans and, to further discourage the birds, have the trash bags liners removed mid-lunch and again immediately following lunch. It is also recommended that the administrators and teachers talk with the students about the change prior to lunch and remind them during lunch. Lastly, because it puts an extra layer of work on the custodian, it is suggested that a student from the In-school Suspension Classroom assist with the final clean up.
Assessment—follow-up inspections reveal that the campus is much cleaner, teachers and students happier, and, best of all, we only see an occasional bird fly over.

Here is a quick review of the process and documentation used in the PECS program:

PECS Page 1

PECS Sheet

Teacher / Staff: _____, _____

_____, _____

Date sent to SARA team: _____

(Briefly explain the Problem, Effect, Cause, and, if available, possible Solution.)

Problem:

Effect:

1) The teacher and/or staff member will briefly explain the problem, issue, or concern.

2) The teacher and/or staff member shall explain the effect that the issue is having on our school, staff, students, etc.

PECS Page 2

PECS Sheet

Cause:

Solution:

NOTE: Submit the PECS sheet to the ISSCT, AP, VP or other designee. Please feel free to volunteer for the SARA team on this matter. You may inquire about the progress at any time. A resolution will be issued as soon as possible.

3) The staff member shall briefly explain the perceived cause of the problem, issue, or concern.

4) The staff member may offer insights, potential solutions, or strategies for resolving the issue.

5) The staff member submits the PECS sheet to the ISSCT, AP, VP or designee for assessment by the SARA team.

Note: Initially, a <u>drop box</u> may be necessary.

The following is the latest and recommended version of the PECS Program form. Your school may choose to stylize your form differently:

PECS Sheet

Teacher / Staff: _____ , _____

_____ , _____

Date sent to SARA team: _____

(Briefly explain the Problem, Effect, Cause, and, if available, possible Solution.)

Problem:

Effect:

PECS Sheet

Cause:

Solution:

NOTE: Submit the PECS sheet to the ISSCT, AP, VP or other designee. Please feel free to volunteer for the SARA team on this matter. You may inquire about the progress at any time. A resolution will be issued as soon as possible.

Here is a quick review of the process and documentation used in the SARA program:

SARA page 1

SARA Team Exploration Sheet

Team Members: _____ . _____
_____ . _____
_____ . _____
_____ . _____

Date PECS Sheet received: _____ Date completed: _____

Survey:

Analysis:

1) Upon receipt of a concern, the SARA team will conduct a survey of the problem, issue or concern within 5 school days.

2) Next, the team will analyze the findings.

SARA page 2

SARA Resolution Sheet

Response:

Assessment:

Resolution reported to staff on _____ by _____

NOTE: The team conclusion will be presented to the Principal and Leadership Team by a SARA team member. The principal may modify the proposal, or return it to the team for more work or clarification. The final resolution will be reported to the staff by the principal or a designee.

3) After analyzing the findings, the team will propose and draft a mutually decided response.

4) The proposal will be submitted to the principal or a designee for approval and implementation.

5) A designated SARA team member will report back to the staff, and conduct an assessment of the implementation within 10 school days.

The following is the latest and recommended version of the SARA Program form. Your school may choose to stylize your form differently:

SARA Team Exploration Sheet

Team Members: _____ , _____

_____ , _____

_____ , _____

_____ , _____

Date PECS Sheet received: _____ Date completed: _____

Survey:

_____

_____

_____

_____

_____

_____

Analysis:

_____

_____

_____

_____

_____

_____

_____

_____

_____

SARA Resolution Sheet

Response:

_____

_____

_____

_____

_____

_____

_____

_____

_____

_____

Assessment:

_____

_____

_____

_____

_____

_____

Resolution reported to staff on _____ *by* _____

NOTE: The team conclusion will be presented to the Principal and Leadership Team by a SARA team member. The principal may modify the proposal, or return it to the team for more work or clarification. The final resolution will be reported to the staff by the principal or a designee.

Once I was asked by a forward thinking, relationship building high school administrator if the program could be expanded to include students as PECS initiators. I could not think of a reason why the process could or should not be extended to students. How awesome would it be if students were on the lookout for campus hazards and suggested potential fixes? If this is not Problem Based Learning and an opportunity for critical thinking, then I'm confused about their definitions. Of course it would require a good bit of front end loading to ensure students understood the serious nature of the process. Other than that, I believed it could be done. In fact, it would be a great way to help establish buy-in and strengthen relationship bonds. My only problem with the suggestion is I didn't think of it first. PECS and SARA can improve the school's climate of safety and culture of learning.

PUTTING IT ALL TOGETHER

There is no doubt that closing the achievement gap between urban underserved students and their higher performing counterparts is possible. In order to improve, several realities must be accepted and several implementations undertaken. The first reality that must be accepted is that the school environment consists of two variables: a climate and a culture. It is a climate of safety and a culture of learning. The next reality is an understanding that it is necessary for these variables to exist in a hierarchical cyclical order. In other words, the climate of safety fosters a culture of learning, and when a culture of learning is in place, it promotes a climate of safety. Together, these entities bring about environmental stabilization. If this understanding is accepted, it should be relatively easy to recognize and accept that in urban underserved school communities, and any other for that matter, the climate of safety precedes the culture of learning.

What distinguishes a high performing school from an underserved school is the fact that in higher performing schools, both the climate of safety and culture of learning have usually been established. In most urban underserved schools, however, this is not the case. They frequently struggle to move beyond the battle for a climate of safety. In order to move beyond this skirmish, it is important to recognize that the avenue for change is through relationships and resources. Relationships are divided into two types, leadership and structure. Resources are divided into human and financial capital. Of the two, the focus of this book has been more about relationships.

Leadership is divided into two types, inspirational and instructional leadership. Structure is subdivided into physical and fraternal structure. It is our belief that what is needed in urban underserved schools is a greater abundance of inspirational instructional leaders.

An inspirational instructional leader is a person who can build authentic relationships with students and staff. This person can also properly align the available resources at their disposal, build the necessary supportive structures, and provide quality instruction.

We further believe that three dynamic inputs are necessary for urban underserved students to be successful. The inputs are the people, programs, and posture.

The people are, as mentioned, inspirational instructional leaders. The programs to be selected and implemented must be derived from Maslow's hierarchy of needs. That is, all professional development efforts and other program implementations must draw their impetus from, and be specifically selected to make improvement in, areas of bio-physical, safety, relationship building, academic achievement or esteem, and self-actualization (altruism).

While the people and the programs are concrete, posture is more abstract. Posture, simply put, is the attitude taken by the people while implementing the programs. In order for a school to improve, the notion of the 3P's must be accepted as the most significant input. They must be the guiding principles for all implementations and interventions.

Although there are numerous UE101 school implementations and interventions available, we suggest that eight of these programs be viewed as essential for improvement. The essential programs are a school posture, rules, expectations and BIP, the teacher-student mediation, student-student mediation, the "New" in-school suspension classroom program, and PECS and SARA. These eight structures are instrumental in creating and establishing a climate of safety and a culture of learning and achievement.

Now that a full dialogue and examination have been pursued and many, if not all, stones have been overturned, all that is left to do is put the plan together. The following is a succinct—two part—plan for urban underserved school improvement and student achievement:

Use the Morrison, Blood, and Thorsborne five stages of RJ in schools—gaining commitment/capturing hearts and minds, developing a shared vision, developing responsive and effective practice, developing a whole school approach, and professional relationships/walking the talk—as the urban underserved school macro-plan. Then use the UE101 urban school improvement process (USIP) as the micro-plan. It will stabilize the campus by focusing on a climate of safety and a culture of learning. Next, focus on the maintenance of a balance between relationships and resources as the guiding implementation principle for improvement. Utilize hiring and professional development strategies to attract and produce inspirational instructional leaders. Certify that all professional development programs are selected and implemented based upon their alignment with the stages of Maslow's hierarchy. Create, feature, and support a school posture over and above the mascot and the mission statement. Finally, implement the essential eight UE101 strategies— posture, rules, expectations and BIP, the teacher-student mediation, student-student mediation, the in-school suspension classroom, and PECS and SARA—as part of the normalized standard operating procedures.

Use the diagrams that follow to outline a graphical pathway to developing your school's USIP:

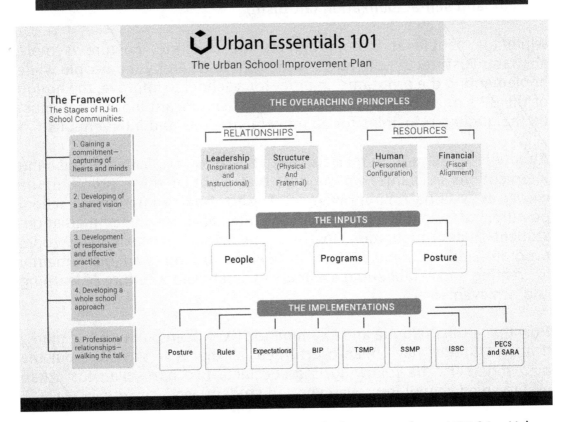

The graphic above is an illustration of the complete UE101, Urban School Improvement Plan (USIP).

STAGES OF RJ IMPLEMENTATION IN SCHOOLS:

Stage 1 : Gaining Commitment—Capturing Hearts and Minds	1. Making a case for a change
	   a. Identifying the need(the cost of current practice)
	   b. Identifying learning gaps
	   c. Challenging current practice
	   d. Debuking the myths around behavior management and what makes a difference
	   e. Linking to other priorities
	 2. Establishing buy-in

Stage 2: Developing a Shared Vision—Knowing where we are going and Why	1. Inspiring a shared vision 2. Developing preferred outcomes aligned with the vision 3. Building a framework for pracrice 4. Developing a common language
Stage 3: Developing Responsive and Effective Practice—Changing how we do things	1. Developing a range of responses 2. Training, maintenance and support 3. Monitoring for quality standrads
Stage 4_ Developing a Whole School Approach—Putting it all together	1. Realingment of school policy with new pracrice 2. Managing the transition 3. Widening the lens
Approach—Putting it all together Stage 5: Professional Relationships—Walking the talk With each other	1. Promoting open, honest, tranparent and fair working relationships 2. Using restorative processes for managing staff grievance, performance management and conflict 3. Challenging practice and behavior-building integrity

The graphic above is an illustration of the Stages of Restorative Justice in School Communities as postulated by Morrison, Blood, and Thorsborne.

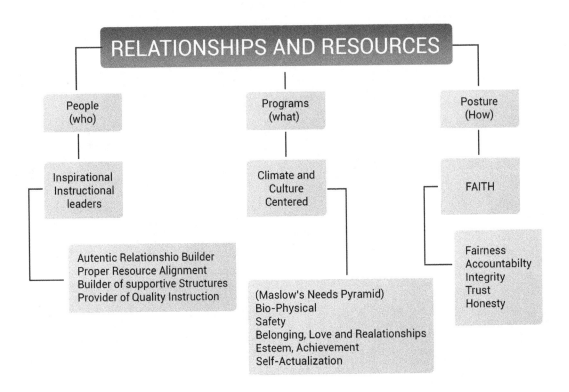

The graphic above is an exploration and illustration of Relationships and Resources, and the process inputs (the 3Ps). The graphic goes on to detail the inputs on a micro-level with greater specification.

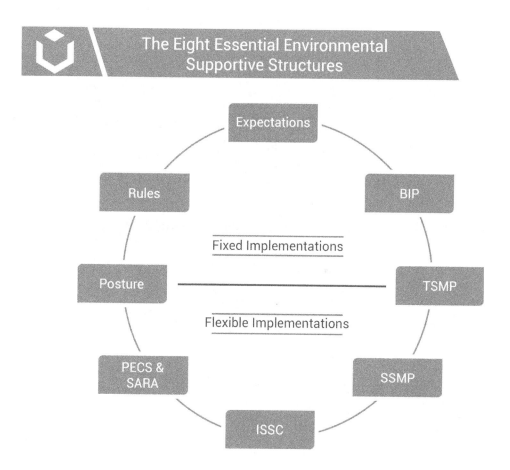

The graphic above is an illustration of the eight (8) essential USIP implementations. It also illustrates the subdivision of the implementations into fixed and flexible structures.

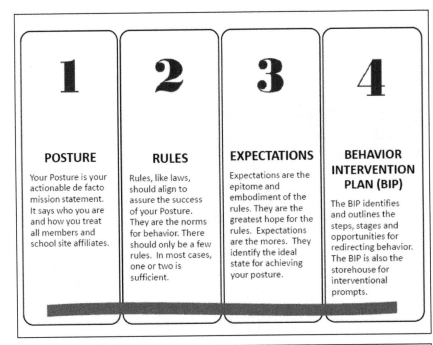

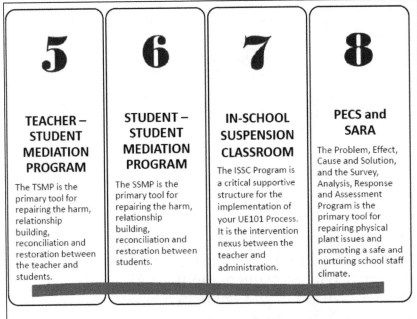

The graphics above are illustrations of the eight (8) essential USIP implementations. In the graphics, the implementation structures are defined and chronologically ordered by execution sequence.

The UE101, Urban School Structure Plan (USIP) can transform your school. All of its implementations and strategies have been fully vetted and determined to be effective in stabilizing urban underserved schools. Now all that is left is for you to unleash its potential on your campus.

GLOSSARY OF UE101 TERMS:

BIP (Behavior Intervention Plan)—A BIP under normal circumstances is an intervention and monitoring protocol for special education students. It is a functional, actionable guideline for managing behavior. It is designed to position a special needs student to receive the best educational services possible. At UE101, when we talk BIP, we mean a behavioral intercession system as part of a comprehensive strategy that includes the entire campus as part of a detailed sequential plan of interventions. The schoolwide BIP comprises the pre-designated actionable corrections and redirections for breaches in the posture, as identified in the rules and expectations. It identifies and outlines the steps, stages, and opportunities for redirecting behavior. The BIP is also the storehouse for interventional prompts.

Campus Legend—A Campus Legend is a veteran teacher or staff member who needs no introduction. It is the person all affiliates know and respect. He or she is the person who is known by students even before they attend the school. The Campus Legend is the teacher who is known for their legendary inspiration. (See legendary inspiration)

Criminal Justice—Criminal justice is a broad term covering topics such as the procedure by which criminal conduct is investigated, evidence gathered, arrests made, charges brought, defenses raised, trials conducted, sentences rendered, and punishment carried out.[51]

Dissimilarity Graphic—the dissimilarity graphic was created by UE101 to highlight the differences between high performing and underperforming schools, and urban underserved students and their teachers. The graphic illustrates the lack of familiarity between the two groups and, therefore, the relationship deficit. It also indicates the low buy-in by the urban underserved student resulting in low behavioral and academic performance.

Expectations—Expectations are the epitome and embodiment of the rules. They are the greatest hope for the rules. Expectations are the academic and behavioral mores. They identify the ideal state for achieving your school posture.

Four Ways to Manage Conflict—There are four ways to handle conflict. At UE101, we designed our program in accordance with the system in place at VORP. We recommend urban underserved schools attempt to apply options number three and four. Option 3 attempts to return power to the parties involved in the conflict with the assistance of a mediator. Option 4 returns all the power to the conflict participants. (See the Options for Handling Conflict graphic)

Inspiration—Inspiration, along with instruction, are the two halves of relationship leadership. Inspiration is defined by Merriam-Webster dictionary as a divine influence or action on a person believed to qualify him or herself to receive and communicate sacred revelation; it is the action or power of moving the intellect or emotion[52]

Instruction—Instruction, along with inspiration, are the two halves of relationship leadership. Instruction includes the knowledge and understanding necessary for the teaching of vital subject content and social behavioral conventions.

ISSC—ISSC stands for in-school suspension classroom. In California, the directive and provisions for the ISSC are in Education Code Section 48911.1.

ISSCT—ISSCT stands for in-school suspension classroom teacher. This position is derived from California Education Code 48 911.1, subsection (c)(1). The section reads as follows: the supervised suspension classroom is staffed as otherwise provided by law.

Jobs—Jobs, as adopted for this book from Ralph Peterson's Life in a Crowded Place, refers to specifically assigned student classroom responsibilities. The number and types of jobs assigned to students in class are limitless. Jobs may include, but are not limited to, book distributor, substitute teacher assistant, greeter, cleanup crew, class reader, technology coordinator and new student orientation specialist. Job assignments are designed to enhance student buy-in and ownership through participation.

Key Accords—The key accords are the primary articles and entities for the conducting of a successful mediation meeting. The key accords are the establishment of mediation ground rules, providing an opportunity for apologies to be made, and a provision for promises to be established.

Legendary Inspiration—At UE101 we created an Urban Education Success Pyramid. The pyramid contains the five relational steps leading to student success. The steps are legendary inspiration, encouragement, self motivation, skill attainment, and achievement. Legendary inspiration is the primary domain and number one duty of the true teacher. It is this teacher, also known as a campus legend, who has the capacity to inspire students to become encouraged and thus begin their journey up the pyramid. It is the teacher or staff member having the capacity to convince a student that he or she is safe and can achieve.

PECS—PECS is an acronym for problem, effect, cause, and solution. PECS is a UE101 program designed to bring physical plant problems or concerns to the forefront. It identifies structural problems and the catalysts for investigation and resolution. Along with the SARA program, which provides a course of action for resolving the problem, PECS addresses physical plant and safety issues in a sequential and timely manner. (See SARA)

Relationships and Resources—Relationships and Resources are the foundational pillars upon which an underserved USIP, or any school plan for that matter, is built on. These titans must be balanced and in a state of constant oversight and equilibrium. It is the balance of relationship and resources that fosters stabilization of the climate and the flourishing of a culture of achievement. Relationships are the routine and ordinary positive interactions between students and community affiliates— parents, doctors, lawyers, teachers, members of the clergy and others. Resources are the human and financial allocations and inputs designed to insure the cultivation and nurturing of positive relationships.

Restorative Justice—Restorative Justice is a theory of justice that emphasizes repairing the harm caused by criminal behavior.[53] RJ views crime as more than breaking the law. It also takes into consideration the harm to the people involved, their relationships, and the community. Restorative justice moves to resolve harms and infringements through mediated reconciliation.

Rites—Rites, as adopted for this book from Ralph Peterson's Life in a Crowded Place, refer to the specific prescribed or customary classroom ceremonies. The purpose of maintaining classroom rites is twofold: intrinsic reward and extrinsic motivation. They serve the same purpose as a bar mitzvah, baptism, or a graduation. Rites are, simply put, momentary pauses to recognize student achievements, task-mastery, or other milestones.

Rituals—Rituals, as adopted from Ralph Peterson's Life in a Crowded Place for this book refer to the prescription for conducting a formal secular ceremony like the ritual of an inauguration. Rituals are the norms and mores of an environment, whether poor or prosperous. They are the formalized routines. Rituals might include greetings, handshakes and the extending of titles (Sir, ma'am, Mr., Ms. and so on). Rituals are critical on the urban underserved campus. Therefore, a huge deal should be made about any deviation from established rituals.

Rules—Rules like laws, should align to assure the success of your Posture. They are the norms for behavior. Rules should be general, and there should only be a few. In most cases, one or two school rules are sufficient. The expectations provide greater specificity of the rules.

SARA—SARA is the acronym for survey, analysis, response, and assessment. SARA is a UE101 program designed to resolve physical plant problems or concerns brought forth by the PECS program. By means of the SARA team, a group of preselected school staff members review all campus physical plant concerns brought forth by the PECS process. They then set out to investigate and offer proposals for a solution, if needed. The process is designed as a means for resolving physical plant and safety issues in a sequential and timely manner. (See PECS)

School Climate—School climate refers to the quality and character of school life. School climate is based on patterns of students, parents, and school personnel's experience of school life and reflects norms, goals, values, interpersonal relationships, teaching and learning practices, and organizational structures. School climate also includes the level of perceived safety. Climate may also be referred to as the temperature of the school.[54]

School Covenant—A school covenant is a file or binder which contains a school's daily operations documents. It contains documents such as the school site plan, the emergency procedures, in California the WASC (Western Association of Schools and Colleges) report, the school's mission statement, posture, rules, expectations, and BIP. The covenant should also contain the operational forms for the TSMP, SSMP, and PECS and SARA programs. This storehouse of materials comes in handy during periods of transition. For example, when there is a change in leadership, the covenant serves as a point to begin procedural discussions.

School Culture—The school culture consists primarily of the underlying values and beliefs that teachers and administrators hold about teaching and learning. The culture is also composed of the traditions and ceremonies schools hold to build community and reinforce their values.[55] School culture is often erroneously used interchangeably with school climate. Maslow's hierarchy of needs may be employed to assist in understanding the difference between the two. The school climate consists of the lower level needs such as biophysical, safety, and love and belonging needs. School culture picks up or begins midway between the love and belonging needs, then proceeds through esteem and self-actualization. It is a climate of safety and a culture of learning and esteem.

School Posture—the school posture is the de facto mission. It is the school's guiding principle. Your school posture is the one thing that all affiliates—teachers, students, staff, parents and other community members—should know, understand, and rally behind. It should be a single word in acronym form that describes your belief and commitment. Your posture should be prominently and prevalently displayed. STRIVE—Safe, Trust, Respect, Inspiration, Vision, and Encourage—is an example of a school posture.

Social Diagnostics—Social diagnostics is a term created by UE101. The term was designed to explain how urban students have acclimated to making assessments of social situations. Many urban students can rapidly diagnose potentially violent or vulnerable situations and respond accordingly. The development of this ability to generate a rapid social diagnosis appears to be related to surviving the hardships of urban underserved communities.

SSMP—SSMP stands for Student- Student Mediation Program. This program was created by UE101. In the student-to-student model, a trained mediator facilitates the process. The process is used to resolve conflict, whether verbal or physical. Because of the importance of the program's effectiveness to the success of the campus environment and culture, the mediator should be the counselor, vice-principal, principal, dean of students, or a designated, trained staff member who is responsible for managing conflict and creating a positive school climate. The mediator's responsibility in the SSMP procedure is to lead the students through mediation in a manner that is safe, fair and restorative for all.

The Five Stages of Restorative Justice in School Communities—The 5 stages of RJ were introduced in the seminal work of Brenda Morrison, Peta Blood, and Margaret Thorsborn, entitled *Practicing Restorative Justice in School Communities: The Challenge of Culture Change.*[56] The stages include gaining commitment, developing a shared vision, developing responsive and effective practice, developing a whole school approach, and professional relationships. This structure was adopted by UE101 as the framework for USIP (Urban School Improvement Plan). It is the guiding structure for the program's overarching principles, inputs, and implementations. (See USIP)

The Urban Essentials—There are five elements that constitute the Urban

Essentials: the student, the environment, discipline, instruction, and the teacher. It is the maintenance and management of these elements and entities that ultimately determine the school site's climate of safety and culture of learning. For a better understanding of the Urban Essentials see *Urban Essentials 101: A Handbook for Understanding and Unleashing the Academic Potential in Urban Underperforming Schools.*

12 Step Mediation Process—This is the UE101 suggested process for mediation. There are 12 steps in the UE101 Mediation Process. The steps are as follows: 1) thank the student for their participation; 2) clearly state the reason for the mediation; 3) clearly state the ground rules for the meeting; 4) acknowledge the student's version of the event; 5) share the behaviors you observed; 6) recognize and address the student's questions and concerns; 7) recognize the student's words on making things right now and in the future; 8) share your position on what would make things right for you; 9) describe explicit instructions for future behavioral and relational expectations; 10) agree on the future expectations; 11) both parties must sign the agreement; and 12) celebrate the mediated resolution agreement.

TSMP—Stands for the Teacher-Student Mediation Program. This mediation model was created by UE101. It is the primary means for resolving staff-to-student conflict in the UE101 process. In the teacher-to-student mediation model, the teacher simultaneously acts as a participant in the process and mediator for the incident. Because of this delicate dual function, it is very important for the teacher to fully understand the mediation process, purpose, and goal. It is easy to see the potential benefits of the program, but it makes abundantly clear the necessity of having highly-skilled, well-qualified professionals involved in the training process.

Underserved Student—Underserved students are defined as students who do not receive equitable resources as other students in the academic pipeline. Typically, these groups of students include low-income, underrepresented racial/ethnic minorities, and first generation students as well as many others[57]

Unmanaged Conflict Cycle—There are five steps in the unmanaged conflict cycle—anxiety or tension, uncertainty or role dilemma, inequity tallying or injustice collecting, altercation or confrontation, and modification or adjustment. This cycle explains what a typical individual experiences when conflict is not effectively managed and mitigated.

Urban School—Urban districts and schools were defined in a study,

A Portrait of Urban Districts and Schools, conducted by the Woodrow Wilson School of Public and International Affairs at Princeton University and the Brookings Institute. Their definition includes the following: urban districts have high shares of poor and minority students. The majority (56 percent) of students in central cities participate in free lunch programs and 40 percent receive services under Title I of the Elementary and Secondary Education Act of 1965. The student population consists of a high number of the nation's immigrant children for whom English is a second language. The share of students classified as limited English proficient is twice as high in central cities as it is in suburbs (17.3 versus 8.2 percent). The students tend to have extremely high rates of mobility, and their community has a higher rate of unemployment, poverty, and crime. Further, the community where the school is located usually suffers from poor "social capital"—the lack of informal connections between people that help a community monitor its children, provide positive role models, and give support to those in need. Lastly, per pupil expenditures are higher, and an eroding tax base makes them unusually dependent on state and federal funding.[58]

Urban Student—Using the definition from the Princeton University and the Brookings Institute study, A Portrait of Urban Districts and Schools, the definition for an urban student is as follows: urban students are typically poor and minority students. They commonly are enrolled in free and reduced lunch programs. They are often Title I, immigrant children, and are English as a Second Language learners. They are the students with high rates of mobility, and their community has high levels of unemployment, poverty and crime. They are the students with limited or poor "social capital"—little community monitoring of its children, few positive role models. As a result, there are frequently higher pupil expenditures, eroding tax bases, and a greater dependence on state and federal funding.

USIP—Stands for Urban School Improvement Plan. It is the model and plan created by Urban Essentials 101 to address the urban low achievement crisis. The plan consists of a four-part model: 1) the framework; 2) the overarching principles; 3) the inputs; and 4) the implementations. The framework consists of the stages of restorative justice in school communities—gaining commitment, developing a shared vision, development of a responsive and effective practice, developing a whole school approach, and the development of professional relationships. The framework is fulfilled through the balancing of the overarching principles of relationships and resources. The relationships and resources plan inputs are the school site's people, programs and posture. The key individual implementations to be managed and monitored by the inputs are the school site's posture, rules, expectations, BIP, TSMP, SSMP, ISSC, and PECS and SARA programs.

VORP—VORP stands for Victim Offender Reconciliation Program. VORP is a restorative approach that brings offenders and their victims face-to-face in an effort to resolve their issues. The process is facilitated by a trained mediator, who is usually a community volunteer. In the process, offenders take meaningful responsibility for their actions and commit to restore the victim's losses. Restitution may be monetary or symbolic. VORP has been established for more than 20 years, and there are thousands of programs worldwide. More than 95% of the cases mediated by VORP result in a written restitution agreement, and over 90% of the agreements are fulfilled within one year. The national rate of reimbursement for non-VORP, court-ordered restitution is 20-30%.[59] The threefold goal of the VORP mediation process—Recognize, Restore, and Future Intentions—were adopted by UE101.

ENDNOTES

1. https://en.wikipedia.org/wiki/Crime_in_Atlanta#History
2. https://en.wikipedia.org/wiki/Crime_in_Atlanta#History
3. https://en.wikipedia.org/wiki/Mechanicsville,_Atlanta
4. https://en.wikipedia.org/wiki/ATL_(film)
5. http://bul.sagepub.com/content/95/1/31.abstract
6. http://www.restorativejustice.org/university-classroom/01introduction
7. http://www.thehistorymakers.com/biography/asa-hilliard-39
8. http://www2.ed.gov/nclb/landing.jhtml
9. http://www.edweek.org/ew/issues/no-child-left-behind/
10. http://www.manta.com/c/mtm953t/elkhorn-correctional-facility
11. http://satellite.tmcnet.com/news/2009/03/25/4082708.htm
12. https://www.biblegateway.com/quicksearch/?quicksearch=right+hand+of+fellowship&qs_version=NIV
13. http://hepg.org/her-home/issues/harvard-educational-review-volume-72-issue-4/herbooknote/the-passionate-teacher_50
14. http://www.urbandictionary.com/define.php?term=snitches+get+stitches!
15. http://www.randomhouse.com/acmart/catalog/display.pperl?isbn=9780679740704
16. http://chicano-park.org/
17. http://sirkenrobinson.com/
18. http://www.wisegeek.com/what-is-the-dance-of-the-lemons.htm#didyouknowout
19. http://en.wikipedia.org/wiki/Searching_for_Bobby_Fischer
20. https://sites.google.com/site/sandiegochessclub/about-us
21. http://www.cde.ca.gov/ta/ac/sa/
22. http://www.cleanlanguage.co.uk/articles/articles/304/1/When-the-Remedy-is-the-Problem/Page1.html
23. http://www.mercedsunstar.com/2013/02/19/2829708/conflict-resolution-for-merced.html
24. http://definitionofleadership.org/
25. http://www.talentmgt.com/articles/eight-principles-of-inspirational-leadership
26. http://educationnext.org/gains-in-teacher-quality/
27. https://www.oecd.org/insights/37966934.pdf
28. http://www.merriam-webster.com/dictionary/conflict
29. http://www.washingtonpost.com/blogs/answer-sheet/wp/2013/12/03/key-pisa-test-results-for-u-s-students/
30. http://www.nytimes.com/2010/12/30/world/asia/30shanghai.html?pagewanted=all&_r=0
31. http://www.oecd.org/pisa/keyfindings/pisa-2012-results-overview.pdf
32. http://www.disabilitymuseum.org/dhm/edu/essay.html?id=42
33. http://www.learning-theories.com/maslows-hierarchy-of-needs.html
34. https://www.probe.org/utilitarianism-the-greatest-good-for-the-greatest-number/
35. http://www.merriam-webster.com/dictionary/posture
36. http://www.disabilitymuseum.org/dhm/edu/essay.html?id=42
37. http://www.leginfo.ca.gov/pub/11-12/bill/asm/ab_1701-750/ab_1729_cfa_20120409_163208_asm_comm.html
38. http://www.legacy.com/news/celebrity-deaths/article/dr-benjamin-spock-child-care-and-controversy
39. http://education.findlaw.com/student-conduct-and-discipline/school-discipline-history.html
40. http://leginfo.legislature.ca.gov/faces/billNavClient.xhtml?bill_id=201320140AB420
41. http://www.merriam-webster.com/dictionary/expectation
42. http://specialchildren.about.com/od/behavioranddiscipline/g/BIP.htm
43. http://www.rtinetwork.org/learn/what/whatisrti

44. http://xroads.virginia.edu/~HYPER2/dewey/ch05.html
45. http://www.merriam-webster.com/dictionary/disciple
46. http://www.merriam-webster.com/dictionary/discipline
47. http://www.leginfo.ca.gov/cgi-bin/calawquery?codesection=edc
48. http://www.cde.ca.gov/ds/fd/ec/currentexpense.asp
49. http://bie.org/about/what_pbl
50. https://www.ncjrs.gov/pdffiles1/nij/grants/224990.pdf
51. http://definitions.uslegal.com/c/criminal-justice/
52. http://www.merriam-webster.com/dictionary/inspiration
53. http://restorativejustice.org/restorative-justice/about-restorative-justice/tutorial-intro-to-restorative-justice/lesson-1-what-is-restorative-justice/
54. http://www.schoolclimate.org/climate/
55. http://www.educationworld.com/a_admin/admin/admin275.shtml
56. http://ibarji.org/docs/morrison.pdf
57. http://media.collegeboard.com/digitalServices/public/School-Counselors-Bridging-the-Gap-Between-College.pdf
58. http://futureofchildren.org/publications/figures-tables/figure_show.xml?fid=111
59. http://www.vorp.com/